TRENDS IN SOUTHEAST ASIA

MUSLIM SECTARIANISM VERSUS THE DE-ESCALATION OF SECTARIANISM IN MALAYSIA

Mohd Faizal Musa

ISSUE
10
2022

Published by: ISEAS Publishing
                30 Heng Mui Keng Terrace
                Singapore 119614
                publish@iseas.edu.sg
                http://bookshop.iseas.edu.sg

ISEAS Library Cataloguing-in-Publication Data

Name(s): Mohd Faizal Musa, author.
Title: Muslim sectarianism versus the de-escalation of sectarianism in Malaysia / by Mohd Faizal Musa.
Description: Singapore : ISEAS-Yusof Ishak Institute, May 2022. | Series: Trends in Southeast Asia, ISSN 0219-3213 ; TRS10/22 | Includes bibliographical references.
Identifiers: ISBN 9789815011562 (soft cover) | ISBN 9789815011579 (pdf)
Subjects: LCSH: Shī'ah—Relations—Malaysia —Sunnites. | Sunnites—Relations—Malaysia —Shī'ah.
Classification: LCC DS501 I59T no. 10(2022)

Typeset by Superskill Graphics Pte Ltd
Printed in Singapore by Mainland Press Pte Ltd

FOREWORD

The economic, political, strategic and cultural dynamism in Southeast Asia has gained added relevance in recent years with the spectacular rise of giant economies in East and South Asia. This has drawn greater attention to the region and to the enhanced role it now plays in international relations and global economics.

The sustained effort made by Southeast Asian nations since 1967 towards a peaceful and gradual integration of their economies has had indubitable success, and perhaps as a consequence of this, most of these countries are undergoing deep political and social changes domestically and are constructing innovative solutions to meet new international challenges. Big Power tensions continue to be played out in the neighbourhood despite the tradition of neutrality exercised by the Association of Southeast Asian Nations (ASEAN).

The **Trends in Southeast Asia** series acts as a platform for serious analyses by selected authors who are experts in their fields. It is aimed at encouraging policymakers and scholars to contemplate the diversity and dynamism of this exciting region.

THE EDITORS

Series Chairman:
   Choi Shing Kwok

Series Editor:
   Ooi Kee Beng

Editorial Committee:
   Daljit Singh
   Francis E. Hutchinson
   Norshahril Saat

Muslim Sectarianism versus the De-escalation of Sectarianism in Malaysia

By Mohd Faizal Musa

EXECUTIVE SUMMARY

- In 1992, a group of academics at the National University of Malaysia (UKM) organized a seminar titled "Seminar Ahli Sunnah dan Syiah Imamiyyah" ("Seminar on Ahl al-Sunnah and Imami Shi'ism") in Kuala Lumpur. It aimed to demonize Shi'a Muslims and ban Shi'ism, effectively escalating sectarianism in Muslim society.
- A Deobandi presenter at the seminar by the name of Muhammad Asri Yusoff put forth arguments about Shi'ism, which later became the "intellectual base" for the discrimination and repression of Shi'a Muslims by Islamic authorities in Malaysia. This repression continues till the present day, and other religious leaders—particularly those with a Salafi orientation—take part in this.
- While much attention has been given to those who have escalated sectarianism, there have also been efforts to de-escalate sectarianism. These efforts come from groups such as Persatuan Ulama Malaysia, and individuals such as Abdul Hadi Awang of PAS, former Prime Minister Mahathir Mohamad, the leader of International Movement for a Just World, Chandra Muzaffar, as well as Malaysian academic, Syed Farid Alatas.
- Nevertheless, the roots of sectarianism have been deeply laid since the seminar in 1992. Unsurprisingly, the sectarian campaign against Shi'as is aligned with the agenda of extremist and terrorist organizations such as ISIS. The sectarian campaign thus arguably emboldens such groups and puts Malaysia and the entire Southeast Asia at risk.

Muslim Sectarianism versus the De-escalation of Sectarianism in Malaysia

By Mohd Faizal Musa[1]

INTRODUCTION

In 1992, a group of academics from the National University of Malaysia (UKM) organized a seminar titled "Seminar Ahli Sunnah dan Syiah Imamiyyah" ("Seminar on Ahl al-Sunnah and Imami Shi'ism") in Kuala Lumpur. The two-day event arguably aimed to demonize the Shi'a sect and its adherents, as evident from the content of the presentations which will be discussed below. Among the various presenters was Wan Zahidi Wan Teh (1992, pp. 1–34), a lecturer from the Department of Shariah who presented a paper on "Ahlul Bait Menurut Pandangan Sunnah dan Syiah" ("The Prophet's Household According to Sunnis and Shi'as").[2] After a lengthy explanation of his own understanding of the *Ahlul Bait*, he argued that Shi'as should not have the right to talk about the *Ahlul Bait*, and he dismissed them as a movement founded by Jews. He then quoted the founder of Wahhabism, Imam Muhammad bin Abdul Wahhab, and referred to Shi'as as apostates (ibid., p. 30). Proclaiming himself as a defender of Islam, he concluded that the goal of Shi'as in Malaysia was

---

[1] Mohd Faizal Musa is Visiting Fellow at the ISEAS – Yusof Ishak Institute, Singapore and Research Fellow at the Institute of the Malay World and Civilization, National University of Malaysia (UKM). He also contributes to the Global Shi'a Diaspora, Project on Shi'ism and Global Affairs at Weatherhead Center, Harvard University.

[2] His paper also appeared in another publication which wrongly stated the year of the seminar as 1993. Refer to Sulaiman Noordin, Mohd Zawawi Abdullah and Mohamad Sabri Haron (2009), pp. 48–83.

to cause Muslims to deviate from the Islamic creed, and to destabilize Muslim society through an underground movement in the country (ibid.).

Another paper titled "Bahaya Syiah Kepada Aqidah, Syariah, Akhlak, Ummah dan Negara" ("The Dangers of Shi'ism to the Islamic Creed, Shariah, Ethics, Muslim Society and the Nation") was presented by a renowned Malaysian Deobandi scholar, Muhammad Asri Yusoff (1992, pp. 4–41).[3] He began his paper by saying that "the truth is that Shi'ism is a teaching that has long been planned and organized by the enemies of Islam. It is the product and fruit of poisonous trees that were planted by Islam's enemies in Muslim lands." Arguably, Muhammad Asri's paper was not presented according to academic conventions. He did not provide any framework or methodology, and his only argument was that Shi'ism was founded by a Jew by the name of Abdullah bin Saba, and is therefore inimical to Islam and Muslims as a whole.[4]

There was only one paper that presented a more objective and balanced view of Shi'ism. In his paper titled "Asal-Usual Syi'ah Imamiah Daripada Perspektif Sejarah dan Budaya Awal Islam Hingga Tahun 40H/660M" ("The Origins of Imamate Shi'ism from the Perspective of the Early History and Culture of Islam to 40H/660CE"), Ismail Abdul Halim examined the similarities between Sunni and Shi'a Islam and stated that both sects believe in Imam Mahdi as the saviour of humankind (ibid., p. 83). Stating that "Muslims today need to look for similarities across the various streams of thought in Islam," he emphasized that there should be an end to the publication of materials which insult any sect

---

[3] This paper also appeared in the above-mentioned publication, on pp. 1–45. It is important to note here that the printed version had been edited and a little toned down. I refer to both versions of the paper when citing it.

[4] This argument has been denounced as untrue, and Shi'as themselves refer to Abdullah bin Saba as an extremist. The presenter further (and falsely) stated that Shi'as perceive Sunnis as impure, and that there are Shi'as who intend to murder Sunnis. He also claimed that allowing Shi'as to freely practise their understanding of Islam would encourage them to make demands for a Shi'a political system based on *Wilayatul Faqih* (guardianship of the jurist), as conceptualized by Imam Khomeini of Iran (ibid., pp. 37–38).

within Islam, be it Sunni Islam, Imami Shi'ism, or Zaydi Shi'ism (ibid.). In fact, he encouraged students in institutes of higher learning to engage in debates on Shi'ism and to understand the historical reasons behind the schisms between the two major sects.

However, it appeared that his arguments and suggestions were not received well, and his paper was not included when UKM published the proceedings of the seminar in 2009 as a book titled *Prosiding Seminar: Syiah Imamiyyah Mazhab ke-5? (Seminar Proceedings: Imami Shi'ism as a Fifth Sect?).*[5]

This seminar is a glaring example of how sectarianism functions. Firstly, although the theme of the seminar was Imami Shi'ism, the organizers did not invite any Shi'a scholars to provide their own perspectives. Thus, there was no engagement with Shi'a representatives. Secondly, almost all of the papers were biased against Shi'ism and presented untrue information about it. Thirdly, the seminar laid the foundations for the development of a harsh attitude towards Shi'ism. In fact, it is possible that Muhammad Asri Yusoff's arguments became the "intellectual base" for the discrimination and repression of Shi'a Muslims by Islamic authorities in Malaysia which continues until today.

The seminar arguably also led to the issuing of a *fatwa* (legal opinion) which completely banned Shi'ism, and this *fatwa* was later gazetted to become part of the law in all states across Malaysia (Mohd Faizal Musa 2020).[6] Released by the Fatwa Committee of the National Council for Islamic Affairs in Malaysia, it was decided that a 1984 *fatwa* accepting the Zaydi and Ja'fari creeds of Shi'ism would be repealed, and that the committee would:

---

[5] While conducting fieldwork for this paper, I was told by a participant of the seminar that Ismail was verbally attacked in a heated discussion during the Question-and-Answer session.

[6] While it is not explicitly stated anywhere that the seminar is what led to the *fatwa* banning Shi'ism, I believe this to be the case. This hypothesis is based on my conversation with Ustaz Din, a former activist from Persatuan Ulama Malaysia, and on my detailed reading of Muhammad Asri Yusoff's presentation at the seminar and its similarity to the points listed in the *fatwa*.

- Determine that the Muslims in Malaysia should only follow the teachings of Islam which [is] based on the beliefs of Sunni Islam in Doctrine, Law and Islamic Morals.
- Support and accept the proposal to amend the Federal Constitution and State Constitutions—to provide expressly that the religion of the Federation and the States shall only be the religion of Islam based on the beliefs of Sunni Islam in Doctrine, Law and Islamic Morals.[7]
- Make provision for amendments to all State Law and Islamic Law to coordinate the Sharia definition of Islamic law to be as follows: "Sharia Law or Islamic law means the Islamic laws based on the beliefs of Sunni Islam in Doctrine, Law and Islamic Morals."
- Recommend that Islamic teachings other than the beliefs of Sunni Islam are contrary to Shariah Law and Islamic Law hence the spread of any doctrine other than that of Sunni Islam is prohibited.
- Stipulate that all Muslims in this country are subject to Islamic Law based on the beliefs of Sunni Islam only.
- Determine that the publishing, broadcasting and distribution of any books, pamphlets, films, videos and others relating to the teachings of Islam which is [sic] opposed to the beliefs of Sunni Islam is prohibited. (Fatwa Committee of the National Council for Islamic Religious Affairs Malaysia 1996.)

This, therefore, marked a turning point for the development of a sectarian mode of thinking in Malaysia, which reached its peak during Najib Razak's administration from 2010 to 2016. During his administration, dozens of Shi'as faced detention without trial, while others were subjected to raids on their private residences and community centres, harassment, book banning, and even an enforced disappearance in 2016, as evident from the case of a Shi'a activist from Perlis, Amri Che Mat. Today, Shi'as are subject to the Shariah Criminal Offenses Act.

---

[7] In Malay, these terms would be *aqidah*, *shariah*, and *akhlak* respectively.

Considering this, it is crucial to understand the roots of sectarianism in Malaysia, and why it persists to this day. This paper examines the development of sectarianism in Malaysia by focusing on the key players and networks involved in propagating sectarian ideas. However, while an understanding of the phenomenon and its manifestation in Malaysia is important, it is equally important to look at existing efforts to de-escalate sectarianism and to promote Islamic ecumenicism. This will be done in subsequent sections of the paper, which introduce key players from different sections of society who have been involved in de-escalating sectarianism.[8]

UNDERSTANDING SECTARIANISM AND ISLAMIC ECUMENICISM

Sectarianism can be defined as "a whole cluster of ideas, beliefs, myths and demonology about religious difference which are used to make religion a social marker, to assign different attributes to various religious groups and to make derogatory remarks about others. It is more than a set of prejudiced attitudes but refers to behaviours, policies and types of treatment that are informed by religious difference" (Jarman 2012, p. 4). According to this definition, sectarianism certainly exists in the Malaysian Muslim context.

Higgins and Brewer (2003, p. 107) argue that sectarianism operates at three levels; as ideas, as individual action, and as a social structure: "at the level of ideas it is expressed in negative stereotypes and pejorative beliefs and language about members of another religion. At the level of individual action, it shows itself in direct discrimination and various types of intimidation and harassment against members of another religion

---

[8] The term "ecumenicism" is commonly understood to be a Christian concept, and may be viewed as inappropriate to be applied in Islamic discourse. However, its use became popular after Rainer Brunner's use of the term to discuss Sunni-Shi'a rapprochement. See Brunner (2004).

because of their group membership. At the social structural level, it expresses itself in patterns of indirect and institutional discrimination and disadvantage."

In the case of Malaysia as described earlier, sectarianism functions on all three levels. The statements made about Shi'ism at the seminar in 1992 and which continue to be propagated till today are proof of the functioning of sectarianism at the level of ideas, and the harassment that Shi'as face in their daily religious life is indicative of sectarianism at the level of individual action. What is most alarming, however, is how sectarianism manifests at the social structural level in the form of raids conducted by religious authorities, and the policies which they introduce.

Morten Valbjørn has argued that "where there is a Sunni/Shi'a divide, sectarianism can be used as part of a range of different kinds of authoritarian techniques" (2019, p. 137). Although Malaysia is a democratic country, the Islamic authorities, who are Sunni, may be said to be manipulating "social dynamics" to stay relevant. This may result in some religious authorities seeking to uphold the status quo to ensure the loyalty of their congregants. For example, in defending the decision to ban Shi'ism, the mufti of Perak reasoned that it is justified as "we are now safe, why do we want to convert to a different sect, this issue arose because there are people among us who are easily influenced and have a tendency to show off" (Faiz Zainudin 2019).

Malaysian religious authorities have also admitted to playing the sectarian card as a "survival strategy", a response to the growing rejection among youths towards institutionalized religion (Valbjørn 2019, p. 141). In order to survive, they peddle untruths about other groups. For example, the Director-General of the Department of Islamic Development Malaysia (JAKIM), Othman Mustapha, claimed that Malaysian Sunnis are attracted to certain lenient aspects of Shi'ism, such as the lack of a requirement to attend Friday prayers, the ability to engage in a contract marriage, the ease of praying three times daily instead of five, and getting married without a dowry (Bernama 2013).

Such statements are untrue allegations, which are indicative of the failure of religious authorities to cross-check their sources, their lack of dialogue with Shi'as, and the absence of critical reasoning. As argued by Ziauddin Sardar and Merryl Wyn Davies (2014, p. 15), these are important criteria to consider in countering sectarianism.[9]

The fanning of sectarianism in the contemporary Muslim world is very much related to the formation of Saudi Arabia in 1744. According to David Commins, "when the first Saudi state (1744 to 1818) conquered much of Arabia in the name of wiping out polytheism, its enemies were other Sunnis (including Hanbalis who rejected Sheikh Muhammad's preaching), recast as infidels according to Wahhabi doctrine. Under the second Saudi state (1824 to 1891), Wahhabi clerics strove to exclude corrupt external influence by declaring a ban on travel to infidel lands, fingering not to Europe, but to neighbouring, mostly Sunni, Arab territories" (2021, pp. 23–26). It was only under the third Saudi state from 1902 that they chose to be more open towards other Sunnis in order to gain recognition from other Muslim nations. They then actively propagated Wahhabism through pan-Islamic missionaries, thus exporting Wahhabism and sectarianism outside their borders. This became especially prevalent after the Iranian Revolution in 1979, which led to Shi'as in Saudi Arabia becoming the victims of repression and discriminatory policies.[10] Consequently, Wahhabism has been misunderstood by some to be mainstream Sunni Islam, while other Muslims such as Shi'as are portrayed as infidels (ibid.).

The opposite of sectarianism is Islamic ecumenicism, which Muslim clerics refer to as *taqrib* (proximity, intra-faith reconciliation, or Sunni-Shi'a rapprochement). For the purpose of this paper, I will refer to it as

---

[9] They are the editors of *Critical Muslims*, a well-known journal based in the United Kingdom. They state that "sectarianism becomes the packaged set of answers that no longer interrogate real questions, and degenerates into customary practice and tradition. Inevitably this signals the end of critical reason about one's own beliefs. In the sectarian worldview it is only the shortcomings of other sects, religions and ideologies that can be critically examined to be found wanting."

[10] In 2006, some Shi'as in Saudi Arabia submitted a petition to the Crown Prince at the time, Fahd Abdul Aziz, which addressed the religious discrimination and poor socio-economic conditions faced by the community. See Fouad Ibrahim (2006), p. 121.

the practice of de-escalating sectarianism. Ibrahim Kazerooni, an imam at the Islamic Center of America and a faculty member of the University of Detroit Mercy explains that the objective of *taqrib* is to "explore the possibility of ground-breaking dialogue that bridges the divide and narrows the divergence that has come to exist between the various schools of thought in Islam" (2021, p. 37).

However, the idea or promotion of *taqrib* is complicated by the policy of the United States (US) in the Middle East. As a result of the presence of the US in the region, some Muslim clerics are receptive to the idea of Islamic rapprochement because sectarianism is the work of the "colonialists, Zionists," and Western powers who "caused the split of the Muslim ummah" (Hersh 2007). Thus, these clerics are more against the colonial agenda of "divide and rule" than they are interested in the proximity between the various schools of thought within Islam. As Kazerooni puts it:

> The importance of the concept of *taqrib* has become urgent especially in the light of the political upheaval ensuing from the occupation of Iraq and the war in Syria, where a unique narrative has gained currency among academics and the general public, which is that the crisis in the Middle East is inherently a sectarian issue that has been there from time immemorial. This kind of narrative not only is factually inaccurate, but also is politically useful for the colonial powers, especially the United States in this case, to deny any responsibility for the crisis of sectarian violence that they themselves have deliberately created as part of the official policy in the region (2021, p. 37).

The project of promoting Islamic ecumenicism is therefore a mammoth effort, as it is connected to the global and regional political order. As Rainer Brunner has stated, it is easier to be a polemicist (and therefore a sectarianist), than to be a conciliator (or a de-escalator of sectarianism) (2021, pp. 15–20).

Furthermore, Muslim clerics who work to promote *taqrib* and "bridgebuilding between various schools of Islam" usually face strong resistance from *takfiri* clerics who are more orthodox and rigid, and who tend to declare other Muslims as apostates. While both groups of clerics organize conferences, publish journals, and hold gatherings for religious leaders from across the Muslim world, the former does so in order to promote bridge building, while the latter disavows such an objective (Kazerooni 2021, p. 40).

In some cases, the tensions between the proponents of *taqrib* and *takfir* have led to violence. For example, a Shi'a cleric by the name of Ayatullah Muhammad Baqir al-Hakim, who was an iconic figure in intra-religious ecumenical projects, as well as a Sunni cleric by the name of Shaykh Muhammad Sa'id Ramadan al-Bouti who was well known for promoting Sunni-Shi'a rapprochement, were both killed by *takfiri* Wahhabi militants from Al-Qaeda and ISIS in 2003 and 2013 respectively (Mohammad Sagha 2021, pp. 45–46).[11]

While such violence may not be prevalent among Muslims in Southeast Asia, there is certainly tension between the *taqrib* and *takfiri* groups in Malaysia, which has also had an impact on Muslims in Singapore.[12]

THE MALAYSIAN SECTARIANIST: CONNECTIONS TO SAUDI ARABIA AND PAKISTAN

In 1906, R.J. Wilkinson made the following observation about Malays while he was residing in British Malaya:

> The Malays are consequently Sunnites like the Moslems of the Deccan; but Persian influence has been so great throughout India that even the Indian Sunnites have become infected with Shiite

---

[11] While ISIS only emerged into public view in 2014, the acronym, which stands for "Islamic State of Iraq and Syria", was already in use in 2013 when they had expanded into Syria and renamed themselves as such. See *History.com*, 10 July 2017.

[12] For more information, see Nurlaila Khalid (2017).

"heresies". In the Malay Peninsula traces of Shiite influence are visible in the Muharram festivities, in the peculiar respect paid to Ali, Hasan and Husain, and in the tone of much of the old Malay Literature. In the matter of religious law the Malays are Shafeites. These explanations of the Malay religious stand-point are, however, somewhat technical; the average native of the Peninsula is generally unaware of the existence of rival Musulman sects and of the divergence of his creed from the truer Sunnite beliefs (1957, pp. 1–2).

He therefore made the observation that Malays paid little attention to the intra-religious differences between them. Up until the establishment of JAKIM, sectarianism was not an issue in Malaysia. It was not uncommon for Muslims to change their school of law when deliberating on a particular issue, and there were Muslim figures who encouraged harmony between Sunnis and Shi'as.[13]

For example, in 1953, Za'ba, a well-known linguist, writer and religious figure, stated in an article that Muslims should be more tolerant of the different schools of thought, including Shi'ism, and that the Malays

---

[13] As the notable law professor Ahmad Ibrahim put it, "the law as applicable to individual Muslims is personal and hereditary. A man is Hanafi or Shafi'i because his ancestors were so. An adult Muslim is, however, free to choose the law by which he is to be governed and some authorities allow a man to change his school of law in one particular matter if his conscience so permits. The courts in India and Malaysia have allowed a person to change his school of law partially to avoid an inconvenient rule of his own school as shown in the cases of "Mohamed Ibrahim v. Gulam Ahmad, 1 Bom, N.C Rep. 239; Salmah v. Soolong (1878) Kyshe 421; Noordin v. Shaik Noordin (1908) 10 S.S.L.R. 72". Another example would be the case of the Sultan of Kelantan who wanted to keep a pet dog. He sought advice from a cleric by the name of Nik Abdullah Wan Musa, who said that the Sultan can perform *talfik*, or to switch between legal schools within Sunni Islam, if he wished to keep the dog. This was because the Maliki legal school is more lenient with regard to keeping dogs. However, this was opposed by traditional scholars and it led to a long debate on the matter, which even involved Haji Abbas Taha, the Grand Kadhi of Singapore at the time (Nik Abdul Aziz Hj. Nik Hassan 1979, pp. 173–80).

should be more pluralistic in engaging with the various schools of thought (Za'ba 2009, p. 138).[14] Additionally, on 2 October 1960, the leader of Parti Islam Se-Malaysia (PAS), Burhanuddin al-Helmi, in his opening speech for "Kongres Ahli-Ahli Tarikat As-Sufiah Seluruh Malaya" ("All-Malaya Congress for Members of the Sufi Order"), reminded the audience that Muslims need to avoid clashes between Sunnis and Shi'as, as such division is created by "greedy rulers" (Burhanuddin al-Helmi 2005, p. 39).

However, sectarianism eventually developed in Malaysia, and it arguably has its roots in the modern version of the *takfiri* framework of excommunicating other Muslims which has its origins in the formation of Saudi Arabia. As a result of the expansion of Saudi power, the Saudis were able to export Wahhabism to other parts of the world.[15] As Ahmad Fauzi Abdul Hamid has said, "under the guise of ummatic unity, Saudi institutions such as the Rabitah al-'Alam Islami (MWL, Muslim World League) and the World Assembly of Muslim Youth (WAMY) have served as conduits for exporting Wahhabi dogma worldwide. The transmission process in Southeast Asia has been well-documented, penetrating structures of Muslim states, ruling parties, charity associations, non-governmental organizations, Islamist movements and educational networks" (2016, p. 8).[16]

---

[14] Za'ba was a controversial figure and during this period, his books were banned in Perak. He was also accused of disseminating the Mu'tazilite doctrine (Abdullah Hussain and Khalid M. Hussain 2000, p. 12). Za'ba's links with the Ahmadiyyah (Qadiani) community should also be mentioned here. For more information, see Abdul Rahman Abdullah (1998), in particular pp. 171–72.

[15] Wahhabis are also disguised under other labels, such as Salafist, Ahle Hadith, and Ahlus Sunnah (Ahmad Farid 2011, pp. 6–9). See Maszlee Malik (2015), where he names Abdullah Yassin, Hussin Yee, Sofwan Badri, Rasul Dahri, Ismail Omar, Johari Mat, Mohd Asri Zainul Abidin, Hafiz Firdaus, and Mohd Yaakub Mohd Yunus as prominent Salafists of the 1980s and 1990s. Mohd Asri Zainal Abidin (MAZA), who is the mufti of Perlis, has also been labelled a Salafist by Ibrahim Abu Bakar (2007) in the paper. See also Zamihan Mat Zin (2017).

[16] For more on Rabitah al-'alam Islami, see Greg Barton (2009), p. 43.

From a sociological perspective, the Wahhabi approach towards reforming religion and society is considered extreme. Syed Farid Alatas, a prominent Malaysian sociologist who is vocal against sectarianism, has underlined five Wahhabi traits which are indicative of an extremist orientation:

> The main traits of such extremism include the following: intolerance of others, particularly Muslims who disagree with their orientations; overemphasis on rules and regulations at the expense of spirituality; forbidding beliefs and practices allowed by the majority of Muslims; non-contextual; and non-historical interpretation of Qur'an and Hadith, and literalism in the interpretation of texts (Alatas 2009, pp. 9–10).

Intolerance of others, specifically other Muslims, and therefore sectarianism, is therefore an extremist trait. As Sanchita Bhattacharya has put it, "the word sectarianism is derived from sect, which means body of people having varied views within the same religion. Sectarianism means observance of the rules of a particular sect or party, especially in a bigoted or narrow-minded way" (2019, p. 88).

Saudi Arabia has also had an influence on the development of Islam and sectarianism in Pakistan. Alexander Alexiev highlighted that Saudi financial support from the early 1980s had contributed to the establishment of thousands of Ahle Hadith[17] and radical Deobandi religious schools and organizations under government auspices. He argues that this contributed decisively to the "wholesale Islamization of Pakistan and its transformation into a jihadist breeding ground in the last two decades of the twentieth century" (2011, p. 45). Arif Rafiq has also pointed out how "ultimately, the confluence of three nearly concurrent events gave birth to the phenomenon of sectarian violence in Pakistan today: the 1977 coup by General Zia ul-Haq and his subsequent Sunni-

---

[17] According to the International Crisis Group, "almost all the Ahle Hadith madrassas in Karachi were established after the anti-Soviet jihad began in Afghanistan" (2007, p. 8).

tinged Islamization programme; the 1979 Islamic Revolution in Iran and moves by Tehran to export its ideology to Shi'i communities elsewhere; and the 1979 Soviet invasion of Afghanistan and the development of a vast Sunni, later Deobandi, jihadi infrastructure inside Pakistan" (2014, p. 16).[18]

This is crucial information, as Muhammad Asri Yusoff was a Deobandi. He arrived at Darul 'Ulum Deoband, India on 22 September 1977 to pursue his studies, after which he continued his studies at Jamiatul Darul 'Uloom in Karachi, Pakistan. It is important to note here that "Sunni Deobandi militant groups are the driving force for Pakistan's growing sectarian violence. Lashkar-e Jhangvi and the Tehreek-e-Taliban Pakistan seek the official declaration of Pakistan's Shi'a as non-Muslims and work to exterminate large numbers of Shi'a to make the remaining population subservient. While the Ahle Sunnat Wal Jamaat organization also seeks to make Shi'as second-class citizens in Pakistan, it makes greater use of political activities and street agitation to press for its demands" (Arif Rafiq 2014, p. 4). Furthermore, Jamiatul Darul 'Uloom Karachi has been listed as an institution that promotes violent jihad (International Crisis Group 2007, p. 8). It is therefore possible that these factors shaped Muhammad Asri's thinking on intra-Muslim issues. In fact, his earliest publications are laden with sectarian tendencies, in which he focuses on criticizing Shi'ism (Faisal bin Ahmad Shah 2009, p. 175). He continues to propagate this sectarian mode of thinking from the pulpit at his religious school,[19] Darul Kautsar, in Kelantan.

This is problematic, as his views have been adopted by JAKIM. For example, he claimed that Shi'as have their own Qur'an, which is different from the one Sunnis have (1996, pp. 12, 194–200). JAKIM supported this claim, stating that Shi'as believe that "the Qur'an has been distorted,

---

[18] Bhattacharya (2019, p. 90) has further highlighted that "sectarian violence was rife in Pakistan in the 1980s and early 1990s. General Zia ul-Haq's policies and legislation aimed at "Islamizing" Pakistan and were formulated in accordance with an orthodox version of the principles of Sunni Islam, to the exclusion of Sunni Barelvis and Shia Muslims."

[19] Also known as a *pondok* school.

whether in the form of omissions or additions, as well as the belief that the Qur'an contains 17 thousand verses" (JAKIM 2012).[20] Such claims are laughable and illogical,[21] and a simple observation of all the Iranians who have won the International Qur'an Recital Competition organized by Malaysia is enough proof of their knowledge of the Qur'an.[22]

Another claim made by Asri during the seminar at UKM in 1992 was that "the presence of Shi'as will create disunity among Muslims as they believe the Sunnis who hold steadfastly to the Qur'an and Sunnah are non-believers and are worse than the devil." He further claimed that Shi'as believe that it is permissible to murder Sunnis (1996, pp. 28, 31, 34).[23] This was reiterated by the director of the Selangor Islamic Religious Department (JAIS), Muhammed Khusrin Munawi, in the aftermath of a JAIS raid on a Shi'a centre during the commemoration of Ashura on 15 December 2010. This raid on Hauzah ar-Redha in Gombak, Selangor, resulted in the arrest of 200 Shi'as, including a local scholar and a visiting scholar from Iran (*Utusan Malaysia*, 17 December 2010).

---

[20] This view was also adopted by the state of Perak in 2012, and was cited as the foundation for a *fatwa* on the banning of Shi'ism.

[21] For further discussion, see al-Ma'azzi (1405 AH).

[22] At least eleven Shi'as have won the International Qur'an Recital Competition (Majlis Tilawah Al-Quran Peringkat Antarabangsa) which was first held in 1961. It continues to be organized today by JAKIM. Examples of notable winners include the 2015 champion, the late Mohsen Hassani Kargar, who was a Qur'an reciter based at Imam Ali Redza's complex in Mashad, Iran, Mohamad Taghi Morawat (1973), Abbas Salimi Naleeni (1979), Ali Sayyah Gordji (1987), Abbas Emam Jomeh (1990), Mansoor Ghasrizadeh (1992), Ahmad Abu Al-Ghasimi (1993), Mohamad Gandom Najad Toosi (1998), Mas'ud Sayah Gordji (2001, related to the 1987 winner), and Hossein Saeid Rostami Tabrizi (2006). The 2009 winner was Usamah Abdullah, a *muezzin* (one who makes the call to prayer) at Imam Hussein's complex in Karbala, Iraq. The Iranian and Iraqi embassies in Kuala Lumpur confirmed that they are indeed Shi'as, although they emphasized that this was not the most important aspect of being Muslim.

[23] This claim was raised by Perak's deputy mufti, Zamri Hashim, when he wanted to reject calls by Chandra Muzaffar to lift the ban on Shi'ism following the fall of the Barisan Nasional government in 2018.

Such claims are baseless. Commenting on such claims, Syed Farid Alatas firmly stated that:

> Anti-Shi'ite hate speech is supported by assertions about Shi'ism that are simply untruths. For example, Shi'ites are said to have their own Qur'an. This continues to be repeated by anti-Shi'ite propagandists despite the fact that evidence of the existence of a Shi'ite Qur'an has never been produced. It is also said that Shi'ism is a religion created by a Yemeni Jew more than 1,400 years ago in Arabia in order to split the early Muslim community. A director of one of the state religious departments in Malaysia reportedly stated that Shi'ites are "fanatics and a threat to national security". This idea was repeated on various occasions by Malaysia's state-dominated media, although Malaysian security itself had never produced such evidence. The same director is also reported to have said that for the Shi'ites, "the blood of the followers of other faiths is lawful and it means that adherents of the followers of Sunnah Wal Jamaah could be killed." While it is true that there are legitimate doctrinal differences between Sunni and Shi'ite Islam that can be discussed in an open and scholarly manner, the anti-Shi'ite literature originating from Malaysia and elsewhere generally presents a distortion or caricature of Shi'ism and attacks that caricature (2017).

The mufti of Perlis, Mohd Asri Zainal Abidin, also known as MAZA, is also known for his sectarian tendencies. In fact, MAZA appeared on stage together with Muhammad Asri Yusoff at a seminar on "The Dangers of Shi'ism", held at the International Islamic University Malaysia (IIUM) on 3 January 2004. Like many other sermons and presentations delivered by MAZA, the recording of this seminar is available online.[24]

---

[24] The video is titled "Seminar Bahaya Syiah" ("Seminar on the Danger of Shi'ism"), *YouTube*, 1 April 2011, https://youtu.be/TQbAKPS_inQ. There used to be many other similar videos of MAZA on *YouTube*, which are no longer available. What should be noted here is that while MAZA is respected at the international level and perceived as a progressive Muslim scholar, the content of his sermons and lectures delivered in Malaysia illustrate otherwise.

The content of MAZA's anti-Shi'a sermons tends to focus on propagating untruths about Shi'ism and alienating Shi'as. Examples of these sermons that are available online include "Siapa Syiah? Amerika Akan Menyerang Iran?" ("Who are the Shi'as? Will US Attack Iran?", 2011), "Sejarah Pahit Antara Sunni dan Syiah" ("The Bitter History between Sunnis and Shi'as", 2012), "Syiah Adalah Satu Ajaran Yang Sesat" ("Shi'ism is a Deviant Teaching", 2013), "Syiah Semua Sesat, Sebahagian Kufur" ("Shi'as are All Heretics, Many of them are Unbelievers", 2013), and "Pendirian Saya Tentang Syiah" ("My Opinion on Shi'ism", 2019).

One of the topics that MAZA appears to be particularly interested in is that of *qama zani*, or the ritual of self-flagellation as the expression of one's grief for Imam Husayn and how he was murdered during the Battle of Karbala.[25] MAZA argues that this ritual is indicative of the fact that Shi'as are deviant, full of vengeance, and willing to shed blood.[26] However, he conveniently ignores the fact that Shi'a clerics themselves have warned against such harmful self-flagellation, labelling it as extreme. For example, in 1927, Sayyid Muhsin al-Amin al-Amili, a Shi'a cleric from Lebanon residing in Najaf at the time, wrote a pamphlet condemning the ritual.[27]

---

[25] It involves striking one's self with blades and chains so as to feel the pain experienced by Imam Husayn. For more information on the practice, see Nakash (1993).

[26] When MAZA, together with twenty officials from the Perlis Religious Office visited the residence of Amri Che Mat, a Shi'a activist who was abducted in 2015 and still missing till this day, he said that Amri's house was filled with pictures of Shi'a *imams* and that Amri is a threat to national security. He did not clarify what he meant. See "Asri Serang Kehilangan Amri, Kata Syiah Ancam 'Keselamatan Negara'" ("Asri Attacks Amri's Disappearance, Says Shi'ism Threatens 'National Security'"), *YouTube*, 23 January 2018, https://www.youtube.com/watch?v=3yhCy_pNP10&feature=youtu.be. The Malaysian Human Rights Commission (SUHAKAM) on 3 April 2019 referred to the case as the first instance of "enforced disappearance" in the country and its public inquiry into the case concluded that the disappearance was carried out by "agents of the state, namely, the Special Branch, Bukit Aman, Kuala Lumpur" (Kua Kia Soong 2019).

[27] In Arabic, "Al-Tanzih li-a'mal al'shabih".

16

However, such a mode of thinking is not limited to individual religious figures, and is even prevalent among politicians. For example, in 2013, sectarianism intensified when Ahmad Zahid Hamidi, then the Minister of Home Affairs, announced the intention to amend the Constitution such that Sunni Islam would be the only legitimate school of thought. Additionally, during the ruling party's (United Malays National Organization, or UMNO) general assembly that year, UMNO leaders called for the eradication of Shi'as in the country. The assembly was attended by Sheikh Khalid Ali Al-Ghomidi, an imam from Mecca. In his speech after congregational prayers, he praised Malaysia for its efforts to curb the spread of Shi'ism (*Utusan Malaysia*, 8 September 2013, pp. 1, 5).

Anti-Shi'a sentiments and hatred have also permeated into right-wing non-governmental organizations (NGOs) such as Pertubuhan Muafakat Sejahtera Masyarakat Malaysia (Muafakat), which has consistently organized seminars to "educate the public" on the dangers of Shi'ism (Muafakat Malaysia 2013). For example, on 8 September 2013, Muafakat organized a seminar on "Facing the Shi'a Virus". Open to the public and held at a state-owned facility in Kuala Lumpur, they invited the Assistant Secretary of the Ministry of Security and Public Order, Zamihan Mat Zin Al-Ghari, to speak about the topic. He is known for his anti-Shi'a hate speeches.[28]

Another NGO involved in such activities is Yayasan Dakwah Islamiah Malaysia (Islamic Da'wah Foundation of Malaysia, or YADIM). At an event organized by them in the state of Perlis, the head of the Perlis

---

[28] One month later, on 13 October 2013, Zamihan was invited to speak at a seminar co-organized by another NGO, Yayasan Mutiara, and the Office of the Penang Mufti. During the seminar held at Universiti Sains Malaysia, Zamihan said that there was an urgent need to restrict the spread of Shi'a teachings, especially because politicians and corporate leaders were complicit in its spread. He said that their involvement was dangerous as they could influence Muslim society through the spread of ideologies, and even through consumer products. This was among the focal points raised in his recycled paper entitled "Modus Operandi Gerakan Syiah dan Ancamannya Kepada Kestabilan Negara" ("The Modus Operandi of the Shi'a Movement and Its Threat to National Security") (*Sinar Harian* 2013).

State Religious Council (MAIPs), Mohamad Sokri Husin, bragged that they had "spotted" a Shi'a student, thus claiming that even teenagers in schools are not spared from the alleged ills of Shi'ism. A report on the seminar stated that MAIPs and JAKIM, together with YADIM, would subsequently organize a faith consolidation programme to raise awareness about the dangers of Shi'ism (*Sinar Harian*, 27 July 2013).

Ikatan Muslim Malaysia (ISMA) is yet another NGO that organizes such events. They even have a research department on Shi'a issues ("Unit Kajian Isu Syiah"). At a seminar organized on 30 November 2013, titled "Seminar Ancaman Serangan Akidah: Bahaya Syiah dan Liberalisme" ("Seminar on the Threat of the Shi'a Creed: Dangers of Shi'ism and Liberalism"), the president of the above-mentioned research department, Mohamad Ismail, claimed that foreign students from Iran were responsible for spreading Shi'ism in Malaysia.[29]

Even groups which are perceived as more progressive have also been involved in propagating anti-Shi'a sentiments. For example, the Malaysian Islamic Youth Movement (ABIM) applauded the Ministry of Home Affairs for its "effective and swift actions" taken against the Shi'as. Additionally, ABIM conducts seminars with the aim to "help society understand more about Shi'a teachings". For example, the Selangor branch of ABIM reported on their blog that they organized a seminar titled "Pemantapan Aqidah: Syiah itu Islam?" ("Strengthening the Faith: Is Shi'ism Considered as Islam?"), during which they invited Abdullah Din, the deputy president of the Kedah branch of the organization, to speak to a large crowd. One of the pictures on that same blog post was accompanied by the caption "anti-Shi'a seminar received encouraging reception".[30]

---

[29] The accusation that foreign traders and students from Iran are to be blamed for spreading Shi'ism is not new. For instance, a professor from UKM, Mansor Mohd Noor, called upon religious authorities to "investigate not only the local students, but also the foreign students" with regard to the spread of Shi'ism (*Sinar Harian* 2013). See also *Sinar Harian*, 28 July 2013b.

[30] See Angkatan Belia Islam Malaysia (ABIM) Selangor (2013).

It is worth noting here that the King, who is the Head of State, did not do much to alleviate the situation. Amidst the government-led campaign against Shi'ism in 2013, the King at the time, Yang Di-Pertuan Agong Tuanku Abdul Halim Mu'adzam Shah, called upon all government quarters to pool their resources together in order to address the spread of Shi'ism in Malaysia (Bernama 2013).[31]

Following this, Friday sermons began to dehumanize Shi'as. For example, in a sermon titled "The Shi'ite Virus" scripted by JAKIM and delivered on 29 November 2013, Muslims were warned to comply with the 1996 *fatwa*, and were reminded that they must adhere only to the teachings of Sunni Islam. They were also urged to report to religious authorities if they "suspect, realize or witness for themselves the existence of any party that seeks to spread the teachings of the Shi'ite faith". The sermon emphasized that such efforts were introduced in the name of jihad to "maintain the sanctity of the religion" (JAKIM 2013). The sermon also included fabricated information about Shi'ism, such as allowing the act of sodomy (Hasbullah Awang Chik 2013).[32]

---

[31] This was in stark contrast to the year 2006, for example, when the Yang Di-Pertuan Agong at the time, Syed Sirajuddin Putra Jamalullail, met with Iranian President Mahmoud Ahmadinejad. Bilateral relations between the two countries were well at its peak during this period. See Zarina Othman, Nor Azizan Idris, and Abdul Halim Daud (2020). With regard to the Agong's actions in 2013, it is understood that while he is constitutionally required to act on advice of the Prime Minister on most matters, as he did in this case, he may otherwise choose to act independently on certain issues. For example, in April 2022, the Sultan of Selangor, acting in his capacity as the chairman of the National Council of Islamic Religious Affairs (MKI), announced that JAKIM cannot issue any statement in response to decisions made by the MKI, or to interfere in their decision-making processes. This was in response to discussions on the Tarekat Naqsyabandiyah al-Aliyyah Syeikh Nazim al-Haqqani, which was recognized by the MKI in 2020, and given the green light to practise their beliefs. See Bernama, 9 April 2022.

[32] This allegation has not been supported by any evidence. In fact, Iran, a predominantly Shi'a country, has been admonished by Western human rights bodies for imposing harsh penalties on individuals who engage in sodomy (Human Rights Watch 2012).

THE MALAYSIAN EQUILIBRIST: EFFORTS TO DE-ESCALATE SECTARIANISM

To be sure, efforts have also been made to de-escalate sectarianism in Malaysia. In response to the seminar held by UKM in 1992, another seminar was jointly organized by Persatuan Ulama Malaysia (Ulama Association of Malaysia, or PUM), Majlis Kakitangan Islam Selangor dan Wilayah (Selangor and Wilayah Islamic Staff Council, or MAKKISW) and Gabungan Mahasiswa Islam Se-Malaysia (Malaysian Association of Muslim Students, or GAMIS) on 3 and 4 July 1993. Titled "Seminar Antarabangsa Pendekatan Mazhab Sunni-Syiah Dalam Konteks Kebangkitan Islam" ("International Seminar on Sunni-Shi'a Rapprochement in the Context of Islam Revivalism"), and attended by 600 participants, the seminar sought to counteract the information presented at the UKM seminar. It is worth noting that the seminar was attended by Shi'a clerics from Iran, such as Ayatullah Amini and the late Ayatullah Ali Al-Tashkiri, who both presented papers on de-escalating sectarianism and the significance of sectarianism as a tool used by Western powers to create disunity among Muslim nations (*Harakah* 1993, pp. 12–13).

Another speaker was the late Syed Hussin Habsyi, an Indonesian cleric who was also well known in Malaysia. In his paper entitled "Pendekatan Mazhab Sunni-Syiah (Syarat-Syaratnya)" ("Sunni-Shi'a Rapprochement [The Conditions]"), he stipulated eight steps to combat sectarianism, as briefly stated below:

(1) Sunni-Shi'a dialogue which puts aside politics or any personal agenda; the sole purpose should be to elevate the Qur'an and Sunnah.
(2) Such dialogue should be purely academic and should only involve learned clerics who have knowledge of the Ja'fari (Twelver Shi'ism), Zaidi, Ibadi and Dzohiri legal schools.
(3) One is not to be fanatical towards one's own legal school.
(4) One should not impose one's judgement on others, or compare the validity of one's legal school to another.
(5) One should have the awareness that all legal schools have enemies who are working to find their weakest point in order to bring them down.

(6) One should not include the masses in such discussions, as their lack of theological knowledge may lead to confusion or the spread of misinformation.

(7) One should not discuss the complex concepts and doctrines of other legal schools on one's own.

(8) One should have the awareness that some factions of certain sects are indeed extreme and are not representative of that particular sect (1993, pp. 1–3).

Most importantly, Syed Hussin rejected the *takfiri* approach of excommunicating Shi'as or labelling them as deviant. He emphasized that events such as the seminar at which he was speaking should not be held for the purpose of criticizing others or promoting sectarianism, but should only be held with good intentions in mind.

Abdul Hadi Awang, the current president of PAS, also presented a paper entitled "Ancaman Kuasa Kuffar dan Konspirasi Musuh Islam (Langkah-Langkah Penangkisannya)" ("The Threat of Infidels and Conspiracies from the Enemies of Islam [Steps to Counter It]").[33] In this paper, he stated that "the Muslim ummah must also avoid disputes with one another, including disputes with other sects whether Sunni or Shi'a, and avoid disputes on matters of the caliphate" (1993).[34]

At the end of the seminar, an eighteen-point resolution to promote Sunni-Shi'a rapprochement was produced.[35] The deputy president of PUM concluded the seminar by suggesting that a secretariat be formed

---

[33] The seminar received huge coverage in PAS' sole media organ, *Harakah*, on 25 June 1993 and 9 July 1993.

[34] Nik Abdul Aziz, who was the Chief Minister of Kelantan at the time, also presented a paper on "Peranan Ulamak Dalam Politik, Dalam Konteks Pendekatan Mazhab" ("The Role of Islamic Scholars in Politics, in the Context of Bridging Legal Schools"). His paper also blamed Western powers for sowing hatred between Muslims (*Harakah* 1993, p. 1).

[35] One of the resolutions criticized UKM for being invaded by Western minds and creating disunity. Another resolution emphasized that "the Islamic Revolution in Iran should be treated as a manifestation of global Islamic revivalism, and not simply as the rising up of a single legal school" (*Harakah* 1993, pp. 12–13).

to work on promoting Sunni-Shi'a rapprochement. Additionally, Ahmad Awang, the president of PUM, then gave a press conference, emphasizing that secularism was more dangerous than Shi'ism (Aziz Muda 1993, p. 7).[36]

At this juncture, it is worth discussing Abdul Hadi Awang's presence at the seminar and his wider approach towards anti-sectarianism. As early as 1989, he expressed his fondness for Imam Khomeini, the leader of the 1979 Iranian Revolution, and referred to him as the "Muslim reformer of early 15th Hijri" (1989, p. 5). Under Abdul Hadi Awang's leadership, PAS chose to be on good terms with Iran and distanced itself from Wahhabi and Salafi-led powers. His stand did not change over the years. When the stigmatization of the Shi'as in Malaysia was at its height in 2013, he questioned why there was "a war against the Shi'a sect which has been around for more than a thousand years" and argued that this "strategy of divide and conquer" was a tactic to "save the West and Israel" from Iran's technological advances (2013).[37] In a short Facebook write-up in 2016, he further criticized those Muslims "who bring in the issue of *takfiri* because of the existence of nonsensical ideas which are linked to creed," and denounced government leaders who blindly propagate sectarian ideas (2016).[38] A year later, while discussing PAS'

---

[36] It is worth noting that Ahmad Awang is now the advisor to Amanah, an offshoot political party of PAS.

[37] Because of his opinion on Iran and sectarianism, Abdul Hadi Awang has been criticized by clerics such as MAZA and the mufti before him, Juanda Jaya.

[38] It is worth quoting him at length: "There is also the most contentious aspect of religion, whereby a *fatwa* was issued by scholars from various countries, arguing that Sunnis are obliged to fight Shi'as and that Shi'as are also obliged to fight Sunnis. There are also those who bring in the issue of *takfiri* because of the existence of nonsensical ideas which are linked to creed, or which are directed against those who do not care about religion because their secular ideology rejects God's laws. There are also Muslims who have long drowned in their own ignorance despite practising religion according to their own sects or who have been blindly following the religion since the colonial period, even though they all still pray and practise the basic pillars of Islam, but still do many nonsensical things which do not exist in any sect. All these groups exist among

foreign policy in its relations with international Islamic movements, he reiterated his commitment to "resolve the issue between the Sunnis and Shi'as internally and as brothers in one Muslim family in the matters of pillars and fundamentals, despite the disagreements between its branches" (2017).[39]

Abdul Hadi Awang's approach towards Sunni-Shi'a rapprochement is therefore unique as he navigates between theological arguments and geopolitical relations. This is interesting considering the fact that he obtained his first degree in Islamic Shariah from the Islamic University of Madinah in 1973, followed by a Master's degree in Islamic Political Science from Al-Azhar University in Egypt in 1976.

---

both Sunnis and Shi'as, and have become the target of punitive weapons. On the other side there are official scholars or fake scholars who have risen to listen to the beat of the drums being beaten by government leaders in various countries who are neither Sunni nor Shi'a. Those leaders are only religious during official festive seasons or when they are with the people. When they are with Satan in or outside the country, religion takes a back seat" (2016). The head of the PAS Ulama Council at the time, Datuk Dr Mahfodz Mohamad, welcomed Abdul Hadi's views and explained that "Shi'ism is part of Islam. While there are Shi'a sects which appear different, it cannot be said that they are deviant and so on" (Faiz Zainudin 2016). Mahfodz Mohamad was a former committee member of PUM, the organization which co-organized the seminar in 1993 to de-escalate sectarianism.

[39] He said this in a Facebook post from 20 November 2017: "Turkey has demonstrated its change from being secular and allied with the West and Israel, to moving towards Islam. Additionally, Iran has demonstrated its change from a government which is not tied to fanatical Shi'a jurisprudence in its governance, to a democratic Islamic system which they refer to as *Wilayah Al-Faqih* (guardianship of the jurist). While Arab countries continue to take refuge with the most Salafi of Sunnis, they are actually dictators who have nothing to do with Sunni Islam. As for Russia, its policy is not Islamophobic, unlike America and its allies. What is the reason that we are obliged to be in solidarity with the Islamic group Hamas, the *jihad* (struggle) of the Sunnis and the Shi'a Hezbollah who have become the scapegoats to be easily sacrificed? Let us first unite to face Israel and its allies, and then resolve the issue between the Sunnis and Shi'as internally and as brothers in one Muslim family in the matters of pillars and fundamentals, despite the disagreements between its branches."

Another politician who has played a big role in de-escalating sectarianism is Mahathir Mohamad, the former Prime Minister of Malaysia. Similar to Abdul Hadi Awang, Mahathir argues that sectarianism is a tool used by the "enemies of Islam" (2013).

It is first important to understand that Mahathir differentiates between Iran as a country and Shi'ism as theology. During Mahathir's first period as Prime Minister, bilateral relations between Iran and Malaysia were steady. There were often visits by Iranian diplomats to Malaysia, and a Memorandum of Understanding was even signed when President Mohamad Khatami visited in July 2002. Furthermore, when Hassan Rohani became President in 2013, Mahathir was present at his inauguration ceremony, and expressed optimism that relations between the two countries would further improve (Asmady Idris and Remaly Yusoff 2015, p. 125).[40] It was also in the year 2013 that Mahathir made a joint statement with former President Khatami amid the increasing

---

[40] Asmady Idris and Remali Yusoff (2015) have summarized relations between Malaysia and Iran since the 1980s: "'Heading towards the 1980s and 1990s, the relations had been growing positively. A few official encounters through diplomatic office continuously took place in Kuala Lumpur; these included a meeting between Mr Majid Hedayatzadeh Razri (Iranian ambassador to Malaysia) and Dr Mahathir, the fourth Malaysian Prime Minister, on 11 January 1983, Mr Mohamed Reza Morshed's (Iranian ambassador to Malaysia) visit with the former Malaysian Information Minister, Dato" Mohamad Rahmat on January 18, 1988, and Omer Suleiman al-Hashmi's (Iranian ambassador to Malaysia) visit to seek an audience with the King of Selangor on 22 July 1992. Nonetheless, the most historical moment was the visit by the former President of Iran, Mohammad Khatami (1997–2005) to Malaysia on 21–24 July 2002. During this meeting, another MoU of economic cooperation was signed in the areas of tourism, trade agreement and the agreement on the promotion and the protection of investments. The Khatami's visit to Malaysia indicates that the bilateral relations had grown in maturity, and both governments were full of enthusiasm to venture into various economic activities. The most notable diplomatic activities are the former Malaysian Prime Minister Abdullah Ahmad Badawi's two-day visit to Tehran on 21–22 December 2008 to sign three agreements on cooperation in technology, anti-drug campaign and car manufacturing, and also Tun Dr Mahathir's presence in Hassan Rohani's inauguration ceremony as the new President of Iran on 4 August 2013. During this visit, Tun Dr Mahathir congratulated the

persecution of Shi'as in Malaysia. Initiated by Chandra Muzaffar, the president of the NGO International Movement for a Just World (JUST), the part of the statement read:

Sunni-Shi'a animosity and antagonism have clearly weakened the Muslim ummah. It has made us more vulnerable to the manipulations and machinations of outside elements determined to subvert the unity and integrity of the ummah. It has allowed those who seek to establish their hegemonic power over us to succeed in their objectives. It is indisputable that Sunni-Shi'a antagonism and conflicts which have resulted in massacres have tarnished the image and dignity of the ummah in the eyes of the world. Few other occurrences in recent times have had such a negative impact. We appeal to all Sunnis and Shi'as, bound as we are by the same faith in Allah, guided by the same Noble Quran, honouring the same last Messenger of Allah, and facing the same Kiblah, to desist from massacring and killing one another immediately (S. Muhammad Khatami, Mahathir Mohamad and Chandra Muzaffar 2013).

The statement thus illustrates how both leaders had the view that sectarianism has been propagated by hegemonic powers, and that the only way to overcome this would be for Sunnis and Shi'as to work together in order to de-escalate sectarianism and uphold the unity of the global Muslim *ummah*. However, while the statement was circulated

---

new Iranian President on his election to the position and expressed optimism that Tehran-Kuala Lumpur ties would improve in line with the interests of both nations and governments. Although in recent times a number of issues have constantly beleaguered Kuala Lumpur-Tehran interactions, especially as a result of the Malaysian government's harsh stance on Syiah but the relations remain unharmed. Even the call from certain parties to cut off Malaysia's relations with Iran which have been blamed for spreading banned Syiah teachings, Malaysian current Foreign Minister, Datuk Anifah Aman has firmly rejected the call by arguing that the Syiah issue was a domestic matter and to be dealt with internally by the concerned authorities" (2015, p. 125).

online and widely reported locally and internationally, it failed to have any impact on the persecution of Shi'as in the country. Furthermore, despite Mahathir's apparent commitment to encouraging intra-Muslim unity, it should be remembered that the 1996 ban on Shi'ism was issued during his administration, and that he even supported a move initiated by the Chief Minister of Kedah (Mukhriz Mahathir, his son) to ban Shi'ism in the state.[41] Thus, while Mahathir believes that Sunnis should accept Shi'ism as part of Islam (Islam Indonesia 2018), he has said that Shi'ism should not take root in Malaysia (Nur Hasliza Mohd Salleh 2019).

Based on this, it can be argued that Mahathir's motivations in de-escalating sectarianism are motivated by political factors, and not religious or theological ones. This is also evident from his role in organizing the KL Summit in 2019, during which he provoked Saudi Arabia by inviting representatives from Qatar, Turkey, and most significantly, Iran. Viewed as a platform for the formation of a new bloc of Muslim nations, the summit was a source of anger for Saudi Arabia, which had put pressure on Pakistan and other Muslim countries to withdraw from the summit (Prashant Waikar and Mohamed Nawab Mohamed Osman 2020). In response to anger from the Saudis, the Turkish president Recep Tayyip Erdogan emphasized that the summit would be a good platform to "talk freely about our issues, from Islamophobia to terrorism, divisions, internal fights ravaging our region, and sectarian and ethnic conflicts" (*Free Malaysia Today*, 19 December 2019).

The event was met with varying responses in Malaysia. Kua Kia Soong, the advisor to SUARAM, an influential human rights NGO in Malaysia, praised the event, saying that seeing the Iranian President share the same stage with the Malaysian prime minister would give Malaysian Shi'as hope that discrimination and oppression in the Muslim world would be addressed (2019). In contrast, an organization of pro-Saudi clerics known as Pertubuhan Ilmuan Malaysia (iLMU), was not happy. In response to the event, they organized a convention on the Islamic knowledge and invited Syeikh Abdurrahman Ibrahim Al-Rubai'in, the

---

[41] See Hasbullah Awang Chik (2013). See also Mahathir Mohamad (2013a).

Religious Affairs Official at the Saudi embassy in Kuala Lumpur to speak. During this convention, Al-Rubai'in referred to Shi'as as deviants and said that Islamic ecumenicism was a futile effort as Shi'as had their own Qur'an.[42] The convention then ended with six resolutions to curb the spread of Shi'ism in Malaysia, as well as a suggestion to request for the King to intervene. They also sought to recognize only the Organisation of Islamic Cooperation (OIC) as the sole platform for Muslim nations to get together (Wan Faizal Ismayatim 2020).

Chandra Muzaffar himself has also been active in de-escalating sectarianism.[43] A well-known scholar, and leader of JUST, Chandra has emphasized that "Shi'ism has been a major force in shaping Muslim history, philosophy, science and culture", and that the only reason Shi'as are treated badly in Malaysia is because of the religious establishment who "have seen themselves as the protector, the custodian of Islam and Muslims in the country" and who feel the need to "preserve the purity of the Shafi'i legal school" (2005, p. ix).

JUST has been actively working to de-escalate sectarianism through its promotion of the Amman Message as its core theme.[44] Amid the

---

[42] His views are unsurprising, considering that established Saudi clerics uniformly denounce Shi'ism (Doran 2004, p. 46).

[43] See also Chandra Muzaffar (2013a).

[44] The Amman Message is a statement that was issued by King Abdullah II bin Al-Hussein of Jordan in 2004. Following this, in July 2005, he convened an international Islamic conference of 200 of the world's leading Islamic scholars from 50 countries. During this conference, the scholars unanimously issued a ruling on three fundamental issues. Known as the Three Points of the Amman Message, they made the following declarations: (1) All 8 schools of legal thought within Islam are valid. These are Hanafi, Maliki, Shafi'i, Hanbali, Ja'fari, Zaydi, Ibadi, and Thahiri; (2) These different schools of thought have more similarities than differences; (3) Nobody may issue a legal ruling without referring to the methodology of these various schools of thought or without the necessary qualifications. The Three Points were unanimously adopted by the various leaders from the Islamic world during the Organization of Islamic Conference (OIC) summit in Mecca in 2005. Between July 2005 and July 2006, the Three Points were then unanimously adopted by six other Islamic scholarly assemblies,

conflict in Syria between 2012 and 2015, Chandra noted that "the antagonism towards Shi'ites, based on false narratives in Syria, reached a crescendo and there were elements in government circles and NGOs in Malaysia pushing these sentiments". He then emphasized that Malaysia was a signatory to the Amman Message, with leaders such as Anwar Ibrahim and Khairy Jamaluddin signing it (Augustin 2018). However, the efforts initiated by JUST may not always be well received. In 2019, JUST attempted to organize a seminar on "The Amman Message" but was forced to cancel it as a Facebook user had threatened to bomb the venue for the seminar, the International Institute of Advanced Islamic Studies (IAIS). Chandra referred to the user, who commented through the account "Gerakan Banteras Syiah" ("Movement to Stop the Spread of Shi'ism"), as a terrorist threat (2019).

Similar to Abdul Hadi Awang and Mahathir Mohamad, Chandra Muzaffar also views sectarianism as part of the larger problem of Western hegemony, and he is known to be close to Iran and to have made statements criticizing the US, Saudi Arabia, and Israel (IRNA 2018). However, while Chandra Muzaffar has been consistently vocal about the discrimination against Shi'as, his efforts may be hampered by the fact that he is the only known face of JUST. Furthermore, if JUST organizes events, these events tend to be small-scale seminars which are conducted in English, and which are therefore only picked up by the English-language media. Consequently, its efforts may not reach the Malay-speaking masses. Additionally, JUST is not very well known among

---

culminating in the establishment of the International Islamic Fiqh Academy of Jeddah in July 2006 (The Amman Message). The Islamabad Declaration was also issued based on the Amman Message. Adopted by the Thirty-Fourth Session of the Islamic Conference of Foreign Ministers under the purview of the OIC, the declaration reads that "no Muslim, whether he or she is Shi'ite or Sunni, may be subject to murder or any harm, intimidation, terrorization, or aggression on his property; incitement thereto; or forcible displacement, deportation or kidnapping. All Muslims are to refrain seriously from any provocation of sensitivities or sectarian or ethnic strife, as well as any name-calling, abuse, prejudice or vilification and invectives" (Islamabad Declaration 2007, pp. 91–93).

Malaysian human rights NGOs, and is often absent from meetings with bodies such as the United Nations.

Another individual who has been active in de-escalating sectarianism is Singapore-based Malaysian sociologist, Syed Farid Alatas. While he is an academic like Chandra Muzaffar, Alatas appears to have a significant following among educated youth in Malaysia. Since 2010, Alatas has held several closed-door meetings, during which he engaged with various individuals and organizations to initiate efforts to de-escalate sectarianism and to champion a more sensible and progressive Islam.

Similar to Chandra Muzaffar, Alatas' efforts include correcting misinformation about Shi'ism, and emphasizing that Wahhabism is the force behind sectarianism. However, unlike Chandra, he is not viewed as a champion of Iran on the global stage, or solely as a human rights defender. Instead, he encourages Malaysian authorities and educational institutions to engage with Iran as a civilization or country which has a lot of knowledge to offer. In fact, he has arranged several academic engagements between Malaysian and Iranian university officials. Occasionally, he uses academic settings to remind Malaysians to be more vigilant of Wahhabism and that the discrimination against Shi'as is immoral (Chung 2019).[45] However, while his efforts are important, they can easily be stifled by the fact that he works in an academic setting, unlike the drivers of sectarianism who have more resources at their disposal and who have greater access to the masses.

THE ATTRACTION OF SECTARIANISM

As a recap, it is to be noted here that the UKM seminar in 1992 was organized by Pusat Pengajian Umum, based at UKM, and was held at the Dewan Muktamar in Pusat Islam, Jalan Perdana, Kuala Lumpur. It was a state-sponsored event which was attended by 500 participants, including religious authorities and religious teachers from all states in the country (Sulaiman Noordin 1996, p. x). In contrast, the seminar organized by

---

[45] See also Alatas (2014).

PUM in 1993 was not state-sponsored, and most of its participants were non-partisan clerics. Furthermore, it was supported by PAS, which was an opposition party at the time.

Thus, considering the support that the 1992 seminar received, it is little wonder that it garnered much attention and that the ideas that came out of it were able to take root in mainstream society.[46]

Even the police force is inclined towards sectarian tendencies. Ayob Khan Mydin Pitchay, the principal assistant director of Bukit Aman's Special Branch counter-terrorism unit, said in 2016 that any effort to curb violence, militancy or terrorism tends to be painted as pro-Shi'a. According to Ayob, the Wahhabi militants' approach is to label the authorities as pro-Shi'a, thus making it difficult for the police to catch them, as they do not want to be labelled as such.[47]

Nevertheless, people have expressed their grievances about the ills of Wahhabi ideas. For example, in 2009, mainstream Malay-language newspapers exposed that Wahhabis have been insulting Sunnis, and traditional Sunni clerics have lamented that Wahhabis are creating disunity among Muslims. For example, Mahfuz Muhammad, an official

---

[46] In fact, such ideas have taken root to the extent that similar seminars have continued to be organized. For example, on 21–22 April 2016, UKM organized another conference on Shi'ism, entitled "Seminar Antarabangsa Gerakan Syiah dan Kesannya Terhadap Dunia Islam" ("International Seminar on the Shi'a Movement and Its Impact on the Muslim World"). However, in contrast to the 1992 seminar, this later seminar was not widely reported and attracted poor attendance. Nevertheless, it should be noted that the seminar was co-organized with the Allied Coordinating Committee of Islamic NGOs (ACCIN) as well as Pertubuhan Ikram Malaysia (IKRAM). While ACCIN is known for its exclusivist tendencies, IKRAM is perceived as a more progressive organization. I argue that this is a misperception, and its role in co-organizing this seminar is testament to their exclusivism. See ANNAS Indonesia (2016).

[47] "Apabila kita (polis) dilabel sebagai pro Syiah, darah kita halal dan kita boleh dibunuh. Itu tindakan bahaya. Dan taktik inilah yang digunakan oleh kumpulan pengganas Daesh" (Ayob Khan Mydin Pitchay 2016, p. 10). See also Bernama (2016).

from the Selangor Islamic Council (MAIS) warned authorities to look into the Wahhabis as they are spreading *takfiri* ideas (Roslan Ibrahim and Mohd Fadly Samsudin 2009, p. 4).[48] Even Zamihan Mat Zin, a cleric who has demonized Shi'as, warned that Wahhabis have "encouraged society to spread violence" and that they have resulted in "intensified discrimination against minority groups" (2017, p. 235).[49]

In 2010, Malaysian authorities suspected that Wahhabi militants were recruiting new cadres on Malaysian campuses (*Kosmo*, 28 December 2010). However, these suspicions, and possibly subsequent discoveries, were kept hidden, and there was a sudden outbreak of sectarianism that lasted for almost a decade, de-escalating only temporarily after the 14th General Elections in 2018. One could easily follow the news coverage between 2010 and 2014 to get an idea of how intense the persecution of Shi'as was at that time (see Appendix).

In a 12 November 2014 Federal Government Gazette concerning Anti-Money Laundering, Anti-Terrorism Financing and Proceeds of Unlawful Activities, the Malaysian government listed thirty-nine individuals as being involved in attempts to create violence in Malaysia. They were linked to thirteen organizations that were perceived as Wahhabi, Deobandi, and Jihadi Salafi groups such as Abu Sayyaf, Islamic State, Al-Shabab, Boko Haram, Jemaah Anshorut Tauhid (also known as Laskar 99), and Mujahidin Indonesia Timor.[50] Between 2 May 2014 and 15 January 2016, there were twenty-five arrests involving eighty-four Wahhabi individuals who planned to sow violence in the country (*Utusan Malaysia*, 19 January 2016, p. 15).

---

[48] See also *Utusan Malaysia*, 7 November 2009, p. 11.

[49] Zamihan's thesis has been categorized as consisting of classified information under the Official Secrets Act 1972.

[50] See Federal Government Gazette dated 12 November 2014 on Anti Money Laundering, Anti-Terrorism Financing and Proceeds of Unlawful Activities (Declaration of Specified Entities and Reporting Requirements) Amendment Order 2014.

These concerns and arrests point to one thing: Shi'as pose less of a threat to national security than Wahhabis do. This was articulated by Hishammuddin Hussein, the Minister of Home Affairs at the time, who said that "the Shi'ites are not a threat from a security point of view" (Mazwin Nik Anis and Zulkifli Abdul Rahman 2010). Scholars also share this view. For example, Curtin Winsor Jr. (2007, p. 10) highlights that "Shi'ites do not regard non-Shi'ite Muslims as unbelievers", and that because they comprise such a small portion of the global Muslim population, their numbers "make any project of revolution impractical". Furthermore, their absolute loyalty to the clerical establishment (*marja'*) would make any *jihadi* attempt against the state impossible, unless they receive official dictation to do so.[51]

Yet, Shi'as have become double targets. Not only are they persecuted by the state, but they are also exposed to the risk of terror attacks from Wahhabi militant groups. In 2016, Ahmad Zahid Hamidi, the Minister of Home Affairs at that time, highlighted that between 2014 and 2016, Wahhabi militants were making progress in their plans. These plans included attacking a Shi'a mosque in Kedah, attacking tourist attractions, stealing weapons, and even attempting to abduct national leaders (2016, pp. 8–9). While these efforts were thwarted by the government, they still pose a formidable threat, as they still receive funding from Muslims who believe that Shi'as are infidels and who wish to contribute to ISIS activities in the Middle East (*Malay Mail*, 22 May 2016). There are even videos posted by Malaysian militants living in the Middle East who

---

[51] The late Kallim Siddiqui (1982, p. 349) also explains how Shi'as obey their *marja'* in all aspects of religious life: "In Iran, the Shi'a ulama have had the added responsibility of interpreting their role in view of their theological position that, while the twelfth Imam remains in occultation, the exercise of all power is usurpatory. The ulama were thus put in a position of permanent opposition. This worked well for nearly a thousand years while the Shi'a remained a minority everywhere and power was exercised by Sunni Kings, Caliphs and Sultans."

encourage those living in Malaysia to kill the police and the enemies of Islam, such as Shi'as, by beheading them and stabbing them in the chest (*Free Malaysia Today*, 23 June 2016). Considering all these factors, it is crucial that sectarianism be curbed and de-escalated, so as to prevent further outbreaks of violence and terrorism.

CONCLUSION

There is no question that sectarianism leads to the violation of human rights. In the case of Malaysia, sectarianism and the consequent discrimination against Shi'as have been institutionalized and implemented in a systematic manner.

In 2019, Dr Wan Salim Mohd Noor, a prominent cleric from PUM, who is also the Mufti of Penang, suggested that Malaysia look into teaching a basic introduction on Shi'ism in schools. In an interview with the news platform *Malaysiakini*, he emphasized that education and schools are the keys to ending Shi'aphobia in Malaysia (Loone 2019). Maszlee Malik, then the Minister for Education, voiced his support for the idea (Yasmin Ramlan 2019).

The idea for the basic tenets of Shi'ism to be taught in schools is not a new one. In a lecture entitled "Preliminary Thoughts on the Nature of Knowledge and the Definition and Aims of Education" delivered at King Abdul Aziz University in Jeddah, Syed Muhammad Naquib al-Attas raised the issue (1979, pp. 19–47). The following year, he raised the issue again in his book *The Concept of Education in Islam: A Framework for an Islamic Philosophy of Education*:

> The core knowledge representing the *fardu 'ayn*, integrated and composed as a harmonious unity at the university level as a model structure for the lower levels, and which must invariably be reflected in successively simpler forms at the pre-university, secondary, and primary levels of the educational system throughout the Muslim world, must reflect not only the Sunni understanding of it, but also accommodate the Shi'i interpretation (1981, p. 42).

However, what would have been a progressive move to de-escalate sectarianism was ignored, and today seminars about the alleged ills of Shi'ism are still being organized in Malaysia.[52]

Yet, Islamic ecumenicism is possible as long as Muslim clerics have the desire to understand the root of sectarianism, and to work towards de-escalating it. As Ussama Maksidi put it, it is crucial that sectarianism, as a "modern reality," "be understood before it can be dismantled" (2001, p. 19). While it has been decades since the seeds of sectarianism have been planted in the minds of Muslims in Malaysia, giving rise to concerns that such tendencies would be difficult to uproot, it is worth referring to Seyyed Hossen Nasr's words as a form of motivation to de-escalate sectarianism:

> The response to challenges to Islam must also be based on the most universal and all-encompassing teachings of Islam avoiding narrow sectarianism and opposition within the Islamic world itself, leaving sectarian and theological or juridical disputes to jurists or theologians and religious scholars who have had the necessary training to carry out such debates. Of course, even in their case, the day has come for them to be able to adopt the larger view of Islamic orthodoxy based on the two *shahadahs* and the universality of the teachings which have emanated from the

---

[52] When the raids on Shi'as were at its peak in 2010, Ahmad Fauzi Abdul Hamid criticized the UMNO-Barisan Nasional administration for its politicking and desire to maintain the status quo: "The ideal form and practice of an Islamic curriculum, as conceived for instance by Syed Naguib Al-Attas, remains far-fetched in state-sanctioned Islamic education in Malaysia. The outcome in terms of enforcement of narrowly interpreted religious law against Muslim non-conformists is all too obvious in Malaysia. Whereas Al-Attas' scheme was broad enough to accommodate even Shi'a interpretations of the revealed sciences, Malaysia has been fastidious in instituting pre-emptive action against and punishment of Malay-Muslims who profess the Shi'a variant of Islamic faith deemed to have deviated from the path of Sunni orthodoxy" (2010, p. 52).

Quran and the Hadith of the Prophet and to avoid sectarian in-
fighting (1993, p. 239).

ACKNOWLEDGEMENT

First of all, I would like to thank Sharifah Afra Alatas for her tremendous help while writing this piece. I am also indebted to the Shi'a community in Malaysia, and The Global Shi'a Diaspora, Project on Shi'ism and Global Affairs at Weatherhead Center, Harvard University.

APPENDIX

Summary of Treatment of Shia Muslims in Malaysia on Freedom of Religion, Freedom of Expression, and Cultural Rights, 26 August 1996 – 26 September 2014

	Date	Act	Person/Group Responsible
1.	26 Aug 1996	After a Special Meeting, a series of *fatwas* were released between 1998 and 2012 by various states in Malaysia that placed restrictions on the practice and spread of Shi'ism.[i]	JAKIM (Malaysia Islamic Development Department) Various state governments in Malaysia
2.	21 Oct 1997	Abdullah Hassan was sent to the Kamunting detention camp under section 8(1) of the Internal Security Act 1960.[ii]	Government of Malaysia
3.	22 May 2001	Seven Shi'as were detained for spreading deviationist teachings. Those who were released early were told to renounce their Shi'a faith and revert to Sunni Islam as a precondition. Between October 2000 and January 2001, six Shi'as were also arrested under the Internal Security Act 1960.[iii]	Government of Malaysia
4.	16 Dec 2010	Many Shi'as were arrested in December 2010 by religious authorities, on accusations of threatening national security. As members of the Shi'a community were commemorating the death of the Prophet Muhammad's grandson in an observation known as Ashura, Selangor Islamic Religious Department officers entered the Ali al-Ridha Islamic Center in Seri Gombak and detained 200 Shi'a Muslims.[iv]	Selangor Islamic Religious Department (JAIS) Selayang Municipal Council Malaysian police

5.	9 March 2011	Malaysia officially banned Shi'as from promoting their faith to other Muslims.[v]	Jamil Khir Baharom, Minister in the Prime Minister's Department (in charge of Islamic Affairs)
6.	27 Aug 2011	The advertisement of drinks by a company believed to be owned by a Shi'a was banned and retracted in the state of Melaka, after which the Melaka state government issued a directive to stop an advertisement of a product related to Shi'a teachings. The state of Malacca enforced the ban on Shi'ism in 1997.[vi]	Dato' Seri Mohd Ali Rustam, Chief Minister of Melaka Melaka Islamic Religious Department
7.	25 May 2011	During a celebration to commemorate the Birth of Fatimah Az-zahra,[vii] four Shi'as were detained under the accusation of spreading and recruiting new Shi'a followers.	JAIS Selayang Municipal Council Malaysian police
8.	14 May 2012	At least 20 security forces accompanied Religious Department officers in another mass arrest of Shi'as who were celebrating the birthday of Lady Fatima, the daughter of the Prophet Muhammad, who is highly regarded in Shi'a Islam.[viii]	JAIS
9.	18 July 2013	The state of Kedah was to enforce the 1996 National Fatwa Council ruling that categorizes Shi'a teachings as deviant. State religious authorities would be empowered to act against any individual or organization preaching Shi'ism.[ix]	Datuk Mukhriz Mahathir, Chief Minister of Kedah

continued on next page

APPENDIX — cont'd

	Date	Act	Person/Group Responsible
10.	24 July 2013	Datuk Seri Abdul Rahim Mohamad Radzi, secretary-general of the Home Ministry, announced that Pertubuhan Shi'ah Malaysia (Shi'a Association of Malaysia) is illegal.[x]	Datuk Seri Abdul Rahim Mohamad Radzi, secretary-general of the Home Ministry.
11.	24 July 2013	It was reported in the media that the Negeri Sembilan state government would gazette a ban on the spread of Shi'a teachings to other Muslims. Thus, while Shi'as would be allowed to practise, they cannot preach.	State government of Negeri Sembilan
12.	25 July 2013	Minister in the Prime Minister's Department, Datuk Seri Jamil Khir Baharom, urged all states to issue and gazette an anti-Shia *fatwa*.[xi]	Datuk Jamil Khir Baharom, Minister in the Prime Minister's Department (in charge of Islamic Affairs)
13.	27 July 2013	The state of Pahang gazetted an anti-Shi'a *fatwa*.[xii] On the same day, Registrar of Societies Director-General Datuk Abdul Rahman Othman announced that any form of organization which has any sort of relations with Shi'as is unauthorized.[xiii]	State of Pahang Registrar of Societies Director-General Datuk Abdul Rahman Othman

14.	1 Aug 2013	Minister in the Prime Minister's Department Datuk Seri Jamil Khir Baharom announced that through the Control and Restrictions of Non-Islamic Religions and the Syariah Criminal Offences Fatwa on Collision, individuals involved in the spread of Shi'ism could be prosecuted in civil court.[xiv]	Datuk Jamil Khir Baharom, Minister in the Prime Minister's Department (in charge of Islamic Affairs)
15.	5 Aug 2013	Two Shi'as were arrested, one for being a female homoeopathic practitioner. Twenty officers raided her clinic, seized her books and later arrested her.[xv] *Both were acquitted on 2 January 2014 due to technical reasons.	Perak Islamic Religious Department (JAIPK)
16.	13 Aug 2013	In the state of Perak, provisions were made within the law to arrest Shi'a who possesses Shi'a literature.[xvi]	State government of Perak
17.	8 Sept 2013	The *mufti* of Federal Territories, Datuk Wan Zahidi Wan Teh, proposes that the Malaysian government cut ties with Iran in order to curb the arrival of Iranian tourists and students.[xvii]	Datuk Wan Zahidi Wan Teh Federal Territory Religious Department
18.	9 Sept 2013	Four Shi'a Muslims were arrested in the state of Perak. A media report for that month stated that enforcement authorities had detained 16 people and carried out 120 inspections in connection with those identified to be linked to the dissemination of Shi'a teachings in the country.[xviii]	JAIPK

continued on next page

	Date	Act	Person/Group Responsible
19.	28 Sept 2013	A raid was conducted on a Shi'a centre in Selangor. Religious authorities seized property, a sum of money to be donated to an orphanage, and valuable items belonging to adherents of Shi'ism.[xix]	JAIS
20.	13 Oct 2013	Assistant Secretary of the Security and Public Order Division of the Home Ministry, Zamihan Mat Zin Al-Ghari, argued for the need for a preventive law firm to curb Shi'a teachings in Malaysia.[xx]	Zamihan Mat Zin Al-Ghari, Assistant Secretary of the Security and Public Order Ministry
21.	21 Oct 2013	Abdullah Isa, an Imam of a mosque in Pahang was detained on the suspicion of practising Shi'ism.[xxi] *His trial started on 8 January 2014 and is still ongoing, without any closure.	Ahmad Raffli Abd Malik, Enforcement Chief of Pahang Islamic Religious Department
22.	30 Oct 2013	Three men charged with possession of documents and books on the teachings of Shi'a Islam pleaded not guilty in Syariah court. Together, they were accused of possessing a banner with the name of twelve saints who are considered very important in Shi'ism, 103 copies of the book "Sunni-Shia Dialogue", a document entitled "Tears of Karbala", and various other offences.[xxii] *They were acquitted on 14 February 2014 due to technical reasons.	State Government of Perak

23.	14 Nov 2013	A Dawoodi Bohra Shi'a headquarters in Kelang was raided. [xxiii]	JAKIM Selangor state police
24.	29 Nov 2013	Local mosques across Malaysia were instructed by state religious councils to deliver anti-Shia Friday prayer sermons, consisting of false information about the practices of Shi'as. [xxiv]	JAKIM
25.	4 Dec 2013	The UMNO Youth Movement proposes to define "Muslim" in the Federal Constitution as exclusively referring to Sunni Islam (*sunnah wal jamaah*). [xxv]	UMNO Youth Movement
26.	5 Dec 2013	The Home Minister of Malaysia, Datuk Seri Dr Ahmad Zahid Hamidi announced that two novels by Faisal Tehrani were to be banned for containing Shi'a Islamic elements, stating that three other books were also to be evaluated, and would soon be banned. [xxvi]	Datuk Seri Ahmad Zahid Hamidi; Home Minister of Malaysia (also the Vice President of UMNO)
27.	6 Dec 2013	During the UMNO general assembly, Datuk Seri Dr Ahmad Zahid Hamidi called for an amendment to the Federal Constitution, with the addition of the words "Sunnah Wal Jamaah" to be inserted after "Islam" as the official religion of Malaysia. This was to curb the spread of and outlaw Shi'a Islam. [xxvii]	Datuk Seri Dr Ahmad Zahid Hamidi, Home Minister of Malaysia
28.	7 Dec 2013	A commission was established to curb deviant teachings, including Shi'ism. [xxviii]	Datuk Seri Dr Ahmad Zahid Hamidi, Home Minister of Malaysia

continued on next page

APPENDIX — cont'd

	Date	Act	Person/Group Responsible
29.	8 Dec 2013	During the UMNO general assembly, Datuk Seri Dr Ahmad Zahid Hamidi claimed that the second leader of opposition party PAS was Shi'a. At this time, Mohammad Sabu was the deputy president of PAS. The Home Minister also proclaimed that he would feel honoured if PAS would support UMNO in their efforts to curb the spread of Shi'a teachings.[xxix]	Datuk Seri Dr Ahmad Zahid Hamidi, Home Minister of Malaysia
30.	10 Dec 2013	The Home Ministry of Malaysia claimed there was evidence to prove that the second leader of PAS was Shi'a. Datuk Dr Seri Ahmad Zahid Hamidi claimed that Mohammad Sabu was a Shi'a disciple. He also gave the green light to JAKIM to take legal action against Mohammad Sabu.[xxx]	Home Ministry of Malaysia Datuk Seri Dr Ahmad Zahid Hamidi, Home Minister of Malaysia
31.	13 Dec 2013	JAKIM claimed that Shi'as were not Muslims.[xxxi]	JAKIM
32.	14 Dec 2013	JAKIM identified 1,500 Shi'a practitioners and asserted their determination to incessantly monitor them and take stern action to curb Shiism.[xxxii]	JAKIM

33.	15 Dec 2013	The Home Ministry announced that they would present to JAKIM all the solid evidence they had linking PAS deputy president Mohamad Sabu to Shi'ism.[xxxiii]	Home Ministry of Malaysia Datuk Seri Dr Ahmad Zahid Hamidi, Home Minister of Malaysia
34.	6 Jan 2014 and 9 Jan 2014	The Home Ministry of Malaysia ordered a prohibition on 12 books on Shi'ism that were allegedly a threat to public order and morality. Any person in possession of those books would be liable under section 8(2) of the Printing Presses and Publications Act 1984 and subject to 3 years imprisonment, or to a fine not exceeding RM20,000, or both.[xxxiv]	Home Ministry of Malaysia
35.	8 Jan 2014	Abdullah Isa was charged with possessing Shi'a material. If found guilty, he could be fined not more than RM2,000, and be imprisoned not more than a year, or both.[xxxv]	Muadzam Shah Syariah Lower Court Pahang Islamic Religious Department
36.	14 Jan 2014	Segamat District Religious Office conducted a thorough investigation to trace the activities of a Shi'a individual allegedly spreading Shi'ism in the area in recent months.[xxxvi]	Segamat District Religious Office
37.	4 Feb 2014	Home Ministry offices and police raided the residence of Khair Izzah Abd Malik and confiscated books (mostly on Shi'a literature) that had been banned. Khair Izzah is the author of the book titled *Meniti Kebenaran* which had also been banned by the Home Ministry of Malaysia.[xxxvii]	Home Ministry of Malaysia Malaysian police

continued on next page

APPENDIX — *cont'd*

	Date	Act	Person/Group Responsible
38.	9 March 2014	28 religious officers together with 100 policemen raided a Shi'a family day occasion to celebrate the birth anniversary of Zaynab al Kubra (Prophet Muhammad's granddaughter) in Selama, Perak. 114 Shi'a followers, including not more than 30 children with the youngest being 3–4 months old, were arrested and spent one night in lock-up. They were given different dates to be interrogated. No charge was made and by 10 March all of them were released on bail.[xxxviii]	Perak Islamic Religious Department (JAIP) Malaysian police
39.	1 April 2014	Datuk Syeikh Muhamad Baderudin Ahmad, the Kedah State Mufti, reportedly proposed the strengthening of the Kedah Sharia Enactment to ensure that no Shi'a followers could escape from Sharia law due to any loopholes.[xxxix] He also added that other states should follow the move.	Kedah State Mufti, Datuk Syeikh Muhamad Baderudin Ahmad
40.	2 April 2014	Abdullah Isa's trial was postponed to 3 June 2014.[xl]	Muadzam Shah Syariah Lower Court Pahang Islamic Religious Department

41.	2 April 2014	In Sandakan, Sabah, Sekong State Assemblyman Datuk Samsudin Yahya branded Shi'ism as deviant and a threat.[xli]	Sekong State Assemblyman Datuk Samsudin Yahya
42.	9 April 2014	The Home Ministry banned the Malay novel *Perempuan Nan Bercinta (A Woman in Love)* by Faisal Tehrani for allegedly containing elements detrimental to public order. The decision was made in order to stop the spread of Shi'a propaganda through creative writings, which were allegedly aimed at academics and teenagers. The prohibition order which took effect on 9 April was in accordance with section 7(1) of the Printing Presses and Publication Act 1984 (Act 301).[xlii]	Malaysian Home Ministry
43.	21 May 2014	The Prime Minister's Religious Advisor, Tan Sri Abdullah Md Zin, claimed that a "second wave of the movement to spread Syiah teachings, which has been linked to extremists, has been detected". He told reporters after opening the International Seminar on Wasatiyyah (Moderate) Approach in Dakwah and Islamic Leadership at Universiti Sains Islam Malaysia (USIM). According to him, the Shi'a "movement" targeted high-ranking individuals at the university level to influence lecturers and students.[xliii]	Prime Minister's Office

continued on next page

45

APPENDIX — cont'd

	Date	Act	Person/Group Responsible
44.	21 July 2014	In Mentakab, in the state of Pahang, religious officers from Pahang Islamic Religious Department raided a Dawoodi Bohra Shia's house for performing "Lailatul Qadr" (last ten odd nights of Ramadan) rituals together. The team, headed by Mohd Anis Mohd Azmi, interviewed 19 men and 13 women.[xliv] They were required to show up at the Pahang Islamic Religious headquarters on 23 July for further investigation.	Pahang Islamic Religious Department
45.	18 Sep 2014	Associate Professor Datuk Mohd Mokhtar Shafii, a member of the Selangor Fatwa Council under the Perak Islamic Religious Department told local Shi'as to move to Iran as there is no place for them in Malaysia.[xlv]	(JAIS)
46.	26 Sep 2014	Malaysian Prime Minister Datuk Seri Najib Tun Razak at the General Debate of the 69th United Nations General Assembly stated that violent extremism and religious intolerance had victimized minorities, including the Shi'as. However, he did not mention anything about Malaysian Shi'as specifically.	Prime Minister of Malaysia

Notes:

[i] *Sinar Harian*, 13 October 2013d.
[ii] *Sinar Harian*, 30 November 2013f.
[iii] *Sinar Harian*, 28 July 2013b.
[iv] *Sinar Harian*, 14 December 2013g.
[v] *New Straits Times*, 28 September 2013.
[vi] JAKIM, 27 February 1998.
[vii] JAKIM, 26 August 1996.
[viii] *Malaysiakini*, 22 May 2001a.
[ix] *Malaysiakini*, 18 June 2001b.
[x] *Harian Metro*, 17 December 2010.
[xi] *Berita Harian*, 9 March 2011.
[xii] *Malaysiakini*, 27 August 2011.
[xiii] *Harian Metro*, 25 May 2011.
[xiv] *Malaysiakini*, 14 May 2012a.
[xv] *Malaysian Insider*, 18 July 2013a.
[xvi] *Malaysian Insider*, 25 July 2013b.
[xvii] *Utusan Arkib*, 25 July 2013a.
[xviii] *Malaysian Insider*, 28 July 2013c.
[xix] *Utusan Arkib*, 13 August 2013b.
[xx] *Sun Daily*, 2 August 2013.
[xxi] *Malaysiakini*, 6 July 2012b.
[xxii] *Utusan Arkib*, 13 August 2013c.
[xxiii] *Utusan Malaysia*, 8 September 2013.
[xxiv] *Utusan Arkib*, 10 September 2013d.
[xxv] *Sinar Harian*, 28 September 2013c.
[xxvi] *Borneo Post*, 24 July 2013.
[xxvii] *Utusan Arkib*, 1 October 2013e.
[xxviii] *Berita Harian*, 14 October 2013a.
[xxix] *Berita Harian*, 22 October 2013b.
[xxx] *Sinar Harian*, 31 October 2013e.
[xxxi] *Harian Metro*, 31 October 2013.
[xxxii] Interview with Sajjad Akhtari. Persatuan Dawoodi Bohra Malaysia. 28 August 2013.
[xxxiii] *My News Hub*, 29 November 2013.
[xxxiv] *Berita Harian*, 4 December 2013c.
[xxxv] *FZ.Com*, 4 December 2013.
[xxxvi] *Malaysiakini*, 5 December 2013.
[xxxvii] *Berita Harian*, 6 December 2013d.
[xxxviii] *Berita Harian*, 7 December 2013e.
[xxxix] *Berita Harian*, 8 December 2013f.
[xl] *Berita Harian*, 10 December 2013g.
[xli] *Malaysian Insider*, 13 December 2013d.
[xlii] Zurairi AR (2014).
[xliii] Bernama, 20 May 2014.
[xliv] Feisal Norawi (2014).
[xlv] Fathin Athirah Hasli (2014).

47

REFERENCES

Abdar Rahman Koya. 2019. "Saudis Unhappy as Dr M Hosts Summit Attended by 'Trio of Enemies'". *Free Malaysia Today*. 18 December 2019. https://www.freemalaysiatoday.com/category/nation/2019/12/18/saudis-unhappy-as-dr-m-hosts-summit-attended-by-trio-of-enemies/

Abdul Hadi Awang. 1989. "Khomeini Sebagai Politikus: Wawancara Khas Al-Ummah Dengan Tuan Guru Haji Abdul Hadi Awang Mengenai Imam Khomeini". *Al-Ummah 21*. July.

———. 1993. "Demi Perpaduan Umat Islam di Rantau Ini: Jangan Sebar Syiah - Ust Hadi". *Harakah* 476. 9 July 1993.

———. 2013. "Kenapa Masalah Sunni dan Syiah Ditimbulkan Sekarang?". *Astro Awani*, 14 December 2013. https://www.astroawani.com/berita-malaysia/kenapa-masalah-sunni-dan-syiah-ditimbulkan-sekarang-26954

———. 2016a. "Iktibar Arab Spring: Politik Matang Dan Sejahtera". *Facebook*, 12 October 2016. https://www.facebook.com/ustaztantawi/posts/10153797773942312

———. 2016b. "Siapa di Sebalik Krisis Syria, Iraq dan Lain-Lain". *Harakah* 2208, 23–25 December 2016.

———. 2017. "Kenyataan Media Presiden Pas Hubungan Intim Arab Dan Israel". *Facebook*, 20 November 2017. https://www.facebook.com/abdulhadiawang/posts/kenyataan-media-presiden-pashubungan-intim-arab-dan-israel-beberapa-media-arab-m/1493563587395421/

———. 2020. "Takziah Atas Pemergian Ayatollah Mohammad Ali Taskhiri". *Twitter*, 19 August 2020. https://twitter.com/abdulhadiawang/status/1295914443814010880

Abdul Rahman Abdullah. 1998. *Pemikiran Islam di Malaysia: Sejarah dan Aliran*. Kuala Lumpur and Penang: DBP and PPPJJ, USM.

Abdullah Hussain and Khalid M. Hussain. 2000. *Pendeta Za'ba Dalam Kenangan*. Kuala Lumpur: Dewan Bahasa dan Pustaka.

AFP. 2011. "Malaysia Shiites Harassed and Face Uncertain Future". 12 February 2011. https://english.alarabiya.net/articles/2011%2F02%2F12%2F137299

Ahmad Farid. 2011. *Al-Salafiyyah: Qawa'id wa Usul*. Alexandria: Dar al-Khulafa al-Rashidun.

Ahmad Fauzi Abdul Hamid. 2010. "Islamic Education in Malaysia". *RSIS Monograph* no. 18. Singapore: S. Rajaratnam School of International Studies.

———. 2016. "ISIS in Southeast Asia: Internalized Wahhabism is a Major Factor". *ISEAS Perspective* no. 2016/24, 16 May 2016. pp. 1–10.

Ahmad Ibrahim. 1965. *Islamic Law in Malaysia*. Singapore: Malaysian Sociological Research Institute Ltd.

Ahmad Zahid Hamidi. 2016. Parliamentary Hansard 13/4. Session 1: 8–9.

Akhtari, Sajjad. 2013. Interview. Persatuan Dawoodi Bohra Malaysia. 28 August 2013.

Al-Attas, Syed Muhammad Naquib. 1980. *The Concept of Education in Islam: A Framework for an Islamic Philosophy of Education*. Kuala Lumpur: Muslim Youth Movement of Malaysia, ABIM.

Al-Ma'azzi, S.K. 1405 AH. *Mushaf al-Qur'an al-Karim*. Tehran: Mu'assassih Intisharat-i Shabirin.

Al-Wardî, Ali. 1956. *Mahzalit al-'Aql al-Basharî/The Comedy of the Human Mind*. 2nd ed. London: Kufaan Publishing.

———. ([1971] 2005). Lamahât Ijtimâ'iyyah min Târîkh Al-'Irâq Al-Hadîth. Vol. 2, 2nd ed. Baghdad, Iraq: Dâr wa Maktabat Al-Mutanabbî.

Alatas, Syed Farid. 2009. "The Study of Muslim Revival: A General Framework". In *Muslim Reform in Southeast Asia: Perspectives from Malaysia, Indonesia and Singapore*, by Syed Farid Alatas. Singapore: Majlis Ugama Islam Singapura.

———. 2014. "Salafism and the Threat to Peace". *Malay Mail*. 10 April 2014. https://www.malaymail.com/news/what-you-think/2014/04/10/salafism-and-the-threat-to-peace-syed-farid-alatas/650241

———. 2017. "Anti-Shi'ite Hate Speech and Managing Sunni-Shi'ite Relations in Singapore". *Karyawan SG*. 15 October 2017. https://karyawan.sg/anti-shiite-hate-speech-and-managing-sunni-shiite-relations-in-singapore/

Alexiev, Alexander R. 2011. *The Wages of Extremism: Radical Islam's Threat to the West and the Muslim World.* Washington, DC: Hudson Institute.

Amman Message. 27 December 2004. http://www.ammanmessage. com/

Anamex87. 2011. "Seminar Bahaya Syiah – Dr Asri (Kertas Kerja 1)". *YouTube.* 1 April 2011. https://youtu.be/TQbAKPS_inQ

Angkatan Belia Islam Malaysia (ABIM) Selangor. 2013. "Syiah Itu Islam?", 19 October 2013, http://abimselangor.blogspot. com/2013/10/syiah-itu- islam.html?m=1

ANNAS Indonesia. 2016. "Resolusi Seminar Anatarabangsa Gerakan Syiah dan Kesannya Terhadap Dunia Islam – Malaysia". 22 April 2016. https://www.annasindonesia.com/read/294-resolusi-seminar-antarabangsa-gerakan-syiah-dan-kesannya-terhadap-dunia-islam-malaysia

Asmady Idris and Remali Yusoff. 2015. "Contemporary Political and Economic Relations with Iran". *International Relations and Diplomacy* 3, no. 2: 123–33.

Augustin, Robin. 2018. "Chandra Calls for Annulment of Anti-Shia Fatwa". *Free Malaysia Today*, 19 November 2018. https://www. freemalaysiatoday.com/category/nation/2018/11/19/chandra-calls-for-annulment-of-anti-shia-fatwa/

Ayob Khan Mydin Pitchay. 2016. "Hapuskan Ideologi Salafi Jihadi Perangi Ancaman Daesh". *Berita Harian*, 12 September 2016.

Aziz Muda. 1993. "Usah Salah Anggap Terhadap Mazhab". *Harakah 476*, 9 July 1993.

Barton, Greg. 2009. "The Historical Development of Jihadi Islamist Thought in Indonesia". In *Radical Islamic Ideology in Southeast Asia*, edited by Scott Helfstein. New York: Department of Social Sciences and an Associate at the Combating Terrorism Center, United States Military Academy at West Point.

Bayat, M. Reza. 2004. "The Malaysia-Iran Relationship: An Observation in the Light of the World's New Era and Post Khatami Foreign Policy". In *Malaysia and the Islamic World*, edited by Abdul Razak Baginda, pp. 157–84. London: ASEAN Academic Press Ltd.

Berita Harian. 2011. "Pengikut Syiah Dilarang Sebar Fahaman,

Bebas untuk Mengamalkan: Jamil Khir". Bernama, 9 March 2011. http://www.bharian.com.my/bharian/articles/ PengikutSyiahdilarangsebarfahaman_bebasuntukmengamalkan_ JamilKhir/Article

———. 2013a. "Gesa Wujud Segera Akta Sekat Syiah". 14 October 2013. http://www.bharian.com.my/bharian/articles/Gesawujud segeraaktasekatSyiah/Article/

———. 2013b. "Imam Amal Ajaran Syiah Akan Didakwa". 22 October 2013. http://www.bharian.com.my/bharian/articles/ ImamamalajaranSyiahakandidakwa/Article/

———. 2013c. "Pemuda Cadang Takrif Islam Sebagai Agama Rasmi Rujuk Pegangan Ahli Sunnah". 4 December 2013. http://www. bharian.com.my/bharian/articles/PemudacadangtakrifIslam sebagaiagamarasmirujukpeganganAhliSunnah/Article

———. 2013d. "KDN Usul Masukkan Perkataan Sunnah wal Jamaah Dalam Perlembagaan". 6 December 2013. http://www. bharian.com.my/bharian/articles/KDNusulmasukperkataan SunnahWalJamaahdalamPerlembagaan/Article/

———. 2013e. "Premis Diguna Pengikut Syiah Akan Disita, Rampas— Zahid". 7 December 2013. http://www.bharian.com.my/bharian/ articles/PremisdigunapengikutSyiahakandisita_rampasZahid/ Article/

———. 2013f. "PAS Perlu Sama Sekat Syiah—Zahid". 8 December 2013. http://www.bharian.com.my/bharian/articles/PAS perlusamasekatSyiah_/Article/

———. 2013g. "KDN Sedia Dedah Siapa Syiah—Zahid". 10 December 2013. http://www. bharian.com.my/bharian/articles/ KDNsediadedahsiapaSyiah/Article/

Bernama. 2013. "Semua Ajaran Syiah di Malaysia Adalah Menyeleweng – JAKIM". *Astro Awani*, 14 December 2013. http://www. astroawani.com/berita-malaysia/semua-ajaran-syiah-di-malaysia-adalah-menyeleweng-jakim-26941

———. 2014. "Second Wave of Syiah Movement Detected". 20 May 2014. http://www.bernama.com/bernama/v7/ge/newsgeneral. php?id=1039835

———. 2016. "Kumpulan Tertentu Dikesan Label PDRM ProSyiah

Untuk Cetus Ketegangan – Polis". 27 January 2016. http://www.
bernama.com/bernama/v8/bm/newsindex.php?id=1210420

———. 2022. "JAKIM Cannot Issue Statements on MKI Decisions –
Sultan of Selangor". *New Straits Times*, 9 April 2022. https://www.
nst.com.my/news/nation/2022/04/787279/jakim-cannot-issue-
statements-mki-decisions-sultan-selangor

Bhattacharya, Sanchita. 2019. "Pakistan: Sectarian War Scourging an
Entire Nation". *Liberal Studies* 4, no. 1: 87–105.

Borneo Post. 2013. "Negeri Sembilan Akan Wartakan Larangan Sebar
Fahaman Syiah". 24 July 2013. http://www.theborneopost.
com/2013/07/24/negeri-sembilan-akan-wartakan-larangan-sebar-
fahaman-syiah/#ixzz2oE9Zjti8

Burhanuddin al-Helmi. 2005. *Simposium Tasauf dan Tarikat Edisi Rumi*.
Ipoh: Pustaka Muda.

Brunner, Rainer. 2004. *Islamic Ecumenicism in the 20th Century: The
Azhar and Shiism between Rapprochement and Restraint*, tr. Joseph
Greenman. Boston: Brill.

———. 2021. "Between Wounded Vanity and Geopolitics: Chances and
Limits of and Islamic Ecumen in the 20th and 21st Centuries". In
*Legacies of Islamic Ecumenicism: Taqrib, Shi'a-Sunni Relations,
and Globalized Politics in the Middle East*. Report May 2021. The
Project on Shi'ism and Global Affairs. Cambridge: Weatherhead
Center for International Affairs, Harvard University.

Chandra Muzaffar. 2005. "Foreword". In *Facing One Qiblah: Legal
and Doctrinal Aspects of Sunni and Shi'ah Muslims*, edited by
Ahmad Kazemi Moussavi, and Karim D. Crow. Singapore: Pustaka
Nasional Pte Ltd.

———. 2013a. "The Syrian Conflict: Qaradawi's Incitement to Violence".
Counter Currents, 3 June 2013. https://www.countercurrents.org/
muzaffar030613.htm

———. 2013b. "Endorse Amman Message on Sunni-Syiah". *The
Star*. 26 December 2013. https://www.thestar.com.my/News/
Nation/2013/12/26/chandra-muzzafar-sunni-syiah-Amman-
Message/

———. 2019. "Stifling the Amman Message with a Bomb Threat".
Malaysiakini, 16 July 2019. https://www.malaysiakini.com/
news/483941

Chung, Nicholas. 2019. "If Sunnis Defend Shias, Politicians Will Champion Shias, Says Academic". *Free Malaysia Today*, 28 September 2019. https://www.freemalaysiatoday.com/category/nation/2019/09/28/if-sunnis-defend-shias-politicians-will-champion-shias-says-academic/

Commins, David. 2021. "Saudi Arabia: Legacies of Taqrib and Takfir". In *Legacies of Islamic Ecumenicism: Taqrib, Shi'a-Sunni Relations, and Globalized Politics in the Middle East*. Report May 2021. The Project on Shi'ism and Global Affairs. Cambridge: Weatherhead Center for International Affairs, Harvard University.

Curtin Winsor, Jr. 2007. "Saudi Arabia, Wahhabism and the Spread of Sunni Theofascism". *Mideast Monitor* 2, no. 1: 1–14. http://www.mideastmonitor.org/issues/0705/0705_2.htm

Doran, Michael Scott. 2004. "The Saudi Paradox". *Foreign Affairs* 83, no. 1. https://www.foreignaffairs.com/articles/saudi-arabia/2004-01-01/saudi-paradox

Faisal bin Ahmad Shah. 2009. "Pelajar-Pelajar Malaysia di Institusi-Institusi Pengajian Islam di India: Analisis Bermula dari Tahun 1947 Sehingga 1990". *Jurnal Al-Tamaddun* 4: 157–76.

Faiz Zainudin. 2016. "Syiah Sebahagian Islam, Kata Ulama PAS". *Free Malaysia Today*. 13 October 2016. https://www.freemalaysiatoday.com/category/bahasa/2016/10/13/sunni-syiah-perlu-bersatu-lawan-musuh-islam-kata-ulama-pas/

———. 2019. "Syiah Tiada Hak Sebar Fahaman di Malaysia, Kata Mufti". *Free Malaysia Today*, 11 September 2019. https://www.freemalaysiatoday.com/category/bahasa/2019/09/11/syiah-tiada-hak-sebar-fahaman-di-malaysia-kata-mufti/

Fathin Athirah Hasli. 2014. "Tiada Tempat Bagi Syiah di Negara Ini". *Sinar Harian*, 18 September 2014. http://www.sinarharian.com.my/semasa/tiada-tempat-bagi-syiah-di-negara-ini-1.317839

Fatwa Committee of the National Council for Islamic Religious Affairs Malaysia. 1996. "Syiah Di Malaysia". http://www.e-fatwa.gov.my/fatwa-kebangsaan/syiah-di-malaysia

Federal Territories Islamic Department. N.d. "Penyelewengan Syiah". In *Mufti Wilayah Persekutuan*. http://www.muftiwp.gov.my/v1/doc/PENYELEWENGANSYIAH.pdf

Feisal Norawi, M. 2014. "Keluarga Syiah Bohra Kena Serbu". *Sinar*

Harian, 21 July 2014. http://www.sinarharian.com.my/semasa/keluarga-syiah-bohra-kena-serbu-1.301565

Fouad Ibrahim. 2006. *The Shi'is of Saudi Arabia.* London: Saqi Books.

Free Malaysia Today. 2016. "Anggota IS Malaysia: Tikamlah Dada Mereka". 23 June 2016. http://www.freemalaysiatoday.com/category/bahasa/2016/06/23/anggota-is-malaysia-tikamlah-dada-mereka/

———. 2019. "Erdogan Takes Veiled Dig at OIC in Speech at KL Summit". 19 December 2019. https://www.freemalaysiatoday.com/category/nation/2019/12/19/erdogan-takes-veiled-dig-at-oic-in-speech-at-kl-summit/

———. 2020. "Syiah Adalah Ancaman, Diplomat Saudi Beritahu Sidang KL". 5 January 2020. https://www.freemalaysiatoday.com/category/bahasa/2020/01/05/syiah-adalah-ancaman-diplomat-saudi-beritahu-sidang-kl/

Funston, John. 2006. "Malaysia: Country Overviews". In *Voices of Islam in Southeast Asia: A Contemporary,* edited by Greg Fealy and Virginia Hooker. Singapore: Institute of Southeast Asian Studies.

FZ.com. 2013. "Youth Proposes to Redefine 'Islam' in the Constitution". 4 December 2013. http://www.fz.com/content/youth-proposes-redefine-islam-constitution

Habsyi, Syed Hussin. 1993. "Pendekatan Mazhab Sunni-Syiah (Syarat-Syaratnya)". In *Prosiding Seminar Antarabangsa Pendekatan Mazhab Sunni-Syiah Dalam Konteks Kebangkitan Islam,* pp. 1–3. Federal Hotel. Kuala Lumpur: Persatuan Ulama Malaysia, MAKKISW and GAMIS.

Halm, Heinz. 1991. *Shi'ism.* Edinburgh: Edinburgh University Press.

Harakah 476. 9 July 1993.

Harian Metro. 2010. "Tatu Kalimah Allah". 17 December 2010. http://www.hmetro.com.my/articles/TatukalimahAllah/Article/

———. 2011. "Markas Syiah Diserbu Lagi". 25 May 2011. http://www.hmetro.com.my/articles/Markassyiahdiserbulagi/Article/

———. 2013. "3 Tidak Mengaku Miliki Barangan Syiah". 31 October 2013. http://www.hmetro.com.my/myMetro/articles/3tidakmengakumilikibaranganSyiah/MA/Article/index_html

Hasbullah Awang Chik. 2013. "PAS Sokong Fatwa Anti Syiah Mukhriz, Minta Kembang Seluruh Negara". *The Malaysian Insider*, 20 July 2013. http://www.themalaysianinsider.com/bahasa/article/pas-sokong-fatwa-anti-syiah-mukhriz-minta-kembang-seluruh-negara

———. 2013. "Khutbah Jumaat: Syiah Haruskan Perbuatan Liwat, Kata Jakim". *The Malaysian Insider*, 29 November 2013. http://www.themalaysianinsider.com/bahasa/article/khutbah-jumaat-syiah-haruskan-perbuatan-liwat-kata-jakim#sthash.MbpxcqUe.dpuf

Hersh, Seymour. 2007. "The Redirection". *The New Yorker*, 25 February 2007. https://www.newyorker.com/magazine/2007/03/05/the-redirection

Higgins, Gareth, and John Brewer. 2003. "The Roots of Sectarianism in Ireland". In *Researching the Troubles: Social Science Perspectives on the Northern Ireland Conflict*, edited by O. Hargie and D. Dickson. Edinburgh: Mainstream Publishers.

History.com. 2017. "ISIS". 10 July 2017. https://www.history.com/topics/21st-century/isis

Human Rights Watch. 2012. "Codifying Repression: An Assessment of Iran's New Penal Code". United States of America: Human Rights Watch. file:///C:/Users/Optiplex-990/Downloads/iran0812webwcover.pdf

Ibrahim Abu Bakar. 2007. "Salafism in Malaysia and Jordan: An Overview". In *International Seminar Proceedings: Issues of Culture and Thought Malaysia-Jordan Perspectives*, edited by Indriaty Ismail, Abdul Rahman Mahmood, Zul'azmi Yaakob, Ahmad Sunawari Long. Department of Theology and Philosophy, National University of Malaysia and Faculty of Syariah, University of Jordan. 26 November 2007.

International Crisis Group. 2007. "Pakistan: Karachi's Madrasas and Violent Extremism". *Asia Report N° 130*. https://www.refworld.org/pdfid/461cd8812.pdf

Islah Perlis. 2012. "(Dr Asri): Sejarah Pahit Antara Sunni Dan Syiah". *YouTube*, 8 January 2012. https://m.youtube.com/watch?v=lVf3JP0lmpg

Islamic Republic News Agency (IRNA). 2018. "Malaysian Scholar Hails Iran as Strong, Influential Country". 11 January 2018. https://

en.irna.ir/news/82792701/Malaysian-scholar-hails-Iran-as-strong-influential-country

Islam Indonesia. 2018. "Mahathir Mohamad: Sunni Harus Menerima Syiah Sebagai Muslim". 1 June 2018. https://islamindonesia.id/berita/mahathir-mohamad-sunni-harus-menerima-syiah-sebagai-muslim.htm

Islamabad Declaration. 2007. Resolution No. 28/34-Pol on Strengthening the Islamic Unity. *The Thirty-fourth Session of the Islamic Conference of Foreign Ministers Session of Peace, Progress and Harmony.* Document file No A/61/981 S/2007./656, 91-93. AFP. 2011.

Ismail Abdul Halim. 1992. "Asal-Usul Syi'ah Imamiah Daripada Perspektif Sejarah dan Budaya Awal Islam Hingga Tahun 40H/660M". Seminar Ahli Sunnah dan Syiah Imemiyyah. 26–27 December 1992. Kuala Lumpur. pp. 76–87.

JAKIM. 1996, "Fatwa Mengenai Ajaran Syiah". 26 August 1996. http://www.e-fatwa.gov.my/fatwa-negeri/fatwa-mengenai-ajaran-syiah

———. 1998. "Ke Arah Membendung Pengaruh Syiah Di Malaysia". 27 February 1998. http://www.e-fatwa.gov.my/fatwa-negeri/ke-arah-membendung-pengaruh-syiah-di-malaysia

———. 2012. "Fatwa Mengenai Pengharaman Ajaran Dan Fahaman Syiah Di Negeri Perak Darul Ridzuan". E-Sumber Maklumat Fatwa. http://e-smaf.islam.gov.my/e-smaf/index.php/main/mainv1/fatwa/pr/10534

Jarman, Neil. 2012. "Defining Sectarianism and Sectarian Hate Crime. European Union's Programme for Peace and Reconciliation (Peace III)". Belfast: Institute for Conflict Research. http://conflictresearch.org.uk/wp-content/uploads/NIACRO-Report-02-Complete-Low-Res.pdf

Karim, Ehsanul. 2007. *Muslim History and Civilization: Modern Day View of Its Histories and Mysteries.* Canada: Pragmatic Publishing.

Kazerooni, Ibrahim. 2021. "The Promises and Challenges of Taqrib". In *Legacies of Islamic Ecumenicism: Taqrib, Shi'a-Sunni Relations, and Globalized Politics in the Middle East.* Report May 2021. The Project on Shi'ism and Global Affairs. Cambridge: Weatherhead Center for International Affairs, Harvard University.

Khairil Ashraf. 2018. "Asri Serang Kehilangan Amri, Kata Syiah Ancam 'Keselamatan Negara'" ("Asri Attacks Amri's Disappearance, Says Shi'ism Threatens 'National Security'"), *YouTube*, 23 January 2018, https://www.youtube.com/watch?v=3yhCy_pNP10&feature=youtu.be

Kosmo. 2010. "Dakwa Universiti Markas Militan". 28 December 2010.

Kua Kia Soong. 2019. "KL Summit Gives Hope to Syiah Minority in Malaysia". *Malaysiakini*, 20 December 2019. https://www.malaysiakini.com/letters/504349

Loone, Susan. 2019. "Mufti P Pinang Saran Pendidikan Atasi Fobia Syiah". *Malaysiakini*. 11 September 2019. https://www.malaysiakini.com/news/491506

Mahathir Mohamad. 2013a. "Kedah Govt to List Shia as Deviant". *New Straits Times*. 19 July 2013. http://www.nst.com.my/nation/general/kedah-govt-to-list-shia-as-deviant-1.322112

_____. 2013b. "Follow Kedah by Gazetting Anti-Shi'a Fatwa". *Malay Mail*, 22 July 2013. http://www.themalaymailonline.com/malaysia/article/follow-kedah-by-gazetting-anti-shia-fatwa

_____. 2013c. "Sunni dan Syiah". *Facebook*, 30 August 2013. https://m.facebook.com/TunDrMahathir/posts/10151624016278652?comment_id=10151627464893652&comment_tracking=%7B%22tn%22%3A%22R%22%7D&refsrc=deprecated&_rdr#_=_

Makdisi, Ussama. "Understanding Sectarianism". *ISIM Newsletter*. https://scholarlypublications.universiteitleiden.nl/access/item%3A2727867/download

Malay Mail. 2016. "Police Freeze Local Bank Account Collecting Funds for IS Militant Group". 22 May 2016. http://m.themalaymailonline.com/malaysia/article/police-freeze-local-bank-account-collecting-funds-for-is-militant-group

MalaysiaDateLine. 2016. "Gerakan Islam Sepakat Bantah Penglibatan Iran, Hizbullah di Syria". 23 December 2016. https://dev.malaysiadateline.com/gerakan-islam-sepakat-bantah-penglibatan-iran-hizbullah-di-syria/

Malaysiakini. 2001a. Group Calls for Release of Shia Muslims Held under ISA". 22 May 2001. http://www.malaysiakini.com/news/3162

———. 2001b. "Use of ISA Against Shia Followers 'UnIslamic and

Unconstitutional'". 18 June 2001. http://www.malaysiakini.com/news/3500

———. 2011. "Melaka Siasat Dalang Sebar Fahaman Syiah". 27 August 2011. http://www.malaysiakini.com/news/174300

———. 2012a. "JAIS Turunkan Kain Rentang di Program Syiah". 14 May 2012. http://www.malaysiakini.com/news/197865

———. 2012b. "Jakim Timbang Haram Novel Dilancar Najib". 6 July 2012. http://www.malaysiakini.com/news/202827

———. 2013. "3 Lagi Buku Sastera Faisal Tehrani Diharamkan". 5 December 2013. http://www.malaysiakini.com/news/248504

———. 2016. "Bekas Mufti 'Kesipuan' Lihat Hadi di Tehran". 19 December 2016. https://www.malaysiakini.com/news/366536

Malaysian Insider. 2013a. "Kedah Mahu Gazet Fatwa Banteras Syiah, kata Mukhriz". 18 July 2013. http://www.themalaysianinsider.com/bahasa/article/kedah-mahu-gazet-fatwa-banteras-syiah-kata-mukhriz (accessed 14 May 2014).

———. 2013b. "Kerajaan-Haramkan-Pertubuhan-Syiah-Malaysia". 25 July 2013. http://www.themalaysianinsider.com/bahasa/article/kerajaan-haramkan-pertubuhan-syiah-malaysia (accessed 14 May 2014).

———. 2013c. "Pahang Warta Fatwa Pengharaman Syiah—Bernama". 28 July 2013. http://www.themalaysianinsider.com/bahasa/article/pahang-warta-fatwa-pengharaman-syiah-bernama (accessed 14 May 2014).

———. 2013d. "Shias Are Not Muslims, Claims Jakim—Bernama". 13 December 2013. http://www.themalaysianinsider.com/malaysia/article/all-branches-of-syiah-teachings-in-malaysia-are-un-islamic-claim-jakim-bern (accessed 14 May 2014).

———. 2014. "Syiah: Ujian Toleransi Agama di Malaysia". 14 February 2014. https://malaysia.news.yahoo.com/syiah-ujian-toleransi-agama-di-malaysia-010126107.html

Manzaidi Mohd Amin. 2016. "Abdul Hadi ke Iran Mewakili Pas". *MalaysiaGazette*, 8 June 2016. https://malaysiagazette.com/2016/12/22/abdul-hadi-ke-iran-mewakili-pas/

Marhaini Kamaruddin. 2008. "Anti-Islam: Jangan Mudah Hukum Barat". *Utusan Malaysia*. 17 February 2008. http://www.utusan.

com.my/utusan/info.asp?y=2008&dt=0217&pub=Utusan_
Malaysia&sec=Dalam_Neg eri&pg=dn_02.htm

Maszlee Malik. 2015. "Salafism in Malaysia: Historical Account on its
Emergence and Motivations". Workshop on Islamic Developments
in Southeast Asia, Singapore, 16 November 2015.

Mazwin Nik Anis and Zulkifli Abdul Rahman. 2010. "Report Ordered
Following Claims of Wahabism and JIL Links". *The Star*. 24 June
2010. 24http://thestar.com.my/news/story.asp?file=/2010/6/24/nati
on/20100624190502&sec=nation

Media Ilmuan Kelantan. 2013. "Syiah; Semua Sesat, Sebahagian Kufur
– Dr Maza". *YouTube*, 22 November 2013. https://www.youtube.
com/watch?v=gNYLb5CVDIU

Mjscbpjnaq. 2011. "Siapa Syiah? Amerika Akan Menyerang Iran? By
Dr. Asri Zainal Abidin". *YouTube*. 28 February 2011. https://www.
youtube.com/watch?v=ayXKBxp12Yo&t=150s

Mohammad Sagha. 2021. "Introduction: Muslim Clergy, Politics, and
the Challenges of Sectarianism in the Middle East". In *Legacies
of Islamic Ecumenicism: Taqrib, Shi'a-Sunni Relations, and
Globalized Politics in the Middle East*. Report May 2021. The
Project on Shi'ism and Global Affairs. Cambridge: Weatherhead
Center for International Affairs, Harvard University.

Mohd Asri Yusof. 1992. "Bahaya Syiah Kepada Aqidah, Syariah, Akhlak,
Ummah dan Negara". Seminar Ahli Sunnah dan Syiah Imemiyyah,
Kuala Lumpur, 26–27 December 1992.

Mohd Faizal Bin Musa. 2013. "The Malaysian Shi'a: A Preliminary
Study of Their History, Oppression, and Denied Rights". *Journal
of Shi'a Islamic Studies* 6, no. 4: 411–62.

———. 2018. "The Riyal and Ringgit of Petro-Islam: Investing Salafism
in Education". In *Islam in Southeast Asia: Negotiating Modernity*,
edited by Norshahril Saat, pp. 63–87. Singapore. ISEAS – Yusof
Ishak Institute.

———. 2020. 'Sunni-Shia Reconciliation in Malaysia'. In *Alternative
Voices in Muslim Southeast Asia: Discourses and Struggles*, edited
by Norshahril Saat and Azhar Ibrahim, pp. 156–82. Singapore:
ISEAS– Yusof Ishak Institute.

———, and Siti Syazwani Zainal Abidin. 2021. "Longer Term External

Conditions Behind Legal Conservatism in Malaysian Islam".
ISEAS Perspective, no. 2021/23, 4 March 2021, pp. 1–9.

———, and Tan Beng Hui. 2017. "State-backed Discrimination Against
Shia Muslims in Malaysia". *Critical Asian Studies* 49, no. 3: 308–
29.

Muhammad Asri Yusoff. 1996. "Bahaya Syiah Kepada Aqidah, Syariah,
Akhlak, Ummah dan Negara". In *Syiah Imamiyah Mazhab ke-5*,
edited by Sulaiman Nordin, Mohd Zawawi Abdullah and Mohamad
Sabri Haron. Kajang: Nuur Publications.

Muhamad Radjab. 2019. *Perang Padri di Sumatra Barat (1803–1838)*.
Jakarta: Balai Pustaka dan Kepustakaan Populer Gramedia.

My News Hub. 2013. "Khutbah Jumaat: Syiah Haruskan Liwat".
29 November 2013. http://mynewshub.my/2013/11/29/khutbah-
jumaat-syiah-haruskan-liwat-jakim/#.Uqyeg_QW3T8

Nakash, Yitzhak. 1993. "An Attempt to Trace the Origin of the
Rituals of ʿĀshūrā'". *Die Welt des Islams: New Series* 33, no. 2:
161–81.

New Straits Times. 2013. "PM's Call at UN: Moderation Can Be Powerful
Tool and Muslims Must Unite Against Those". 28 September 2013.
http://www.nst.com.my/latest/pm-s-call-at-un-moderation-can-
be-powerful-tool-and-muslims-must-unite-against-those-using-
religion-1.364879

Nik Abdul Aziz Hj. Nik Hassan. 1979. "Perbahasan Tentang Jilatan
Anjing: Suatu Perhatian". *Jebat Malaysian Journal of History,
Politics and Strategic Studies* 9: 173–80.

Nur Hasliza Mohd Salleh. 2019. "Syiah Ada Hak Peribadi, Tapi Jangan
Cuba Sebar Ajaran, Kata PM". *Free Malaysia Today*. 11 July 2019
https://www.freemalaysiatoday.com/category/bahasa/2019/07/11/
syiah-bebas-diamal-jika-hormati-fahaman-islam-majoriti-rakyat-
kata-pm/

Nurlaila Khalid. 2017. "Understanding Sunni-Shiite Transitions Among
the First Generation Malay Shiites in Singapore". Master's Thesis,
National University of Singapore.

PROmediaTAJDID Short Video. 2019."Dr Maza—Pendirian Saya
Tentang Syiah". *YouTube*, 16 May 2019. https://m.youtube.com/
watch?v=X8zabPJzWwI

Rafiq, Arif. 2014. "Sunni Deobandi-Shi'i Sectarian Violence in Pakistan Explaining the Resurgence since 2007". *Middle East Institute.* https://www.mei.edu/sites/default/files/publications/Arif%20 Rafiq%20report.pdf

Roslan Ibrahim and Mohd Fadly Samsudin. 2009. "Pengikut Wahabi Sukar Dicam". *Harian Metro.* 6 November 2009.

S. Muhammad Khatami, Mahathir Mohamad and Chandra Muzaffar. 2013. "An Appeal to Sunni and Shia Muslims from Dr Mahathir Mohamad and Sayyid Muhammad Khatami". https://www. countercurrents.org/AJoint%20Appeal%20to%20Sunnis%20 and%20Shias%20(English)%20to%20Editors.pdf

Sardar, Ziauddin, and Merryl Wyn Davies. 2014. "Sectarianism Unbound". *Critical Muslim* 10, no. 1.

Seyyed Hossein Nasr. 1993. *A Young Muslim's Guide to the Modern World.* Kuala Lumpur: Islamic Book Trust.

Shaarani Ismail. 2018. "Fatwa Haram Syiah Tidak Silap—Timbalan Mufti Perak". *Berita Harian*, 20 November 2018. https://www. bharian.com.my/berita/nasional/2018/11/500058/fatwa-haram-syiah-tidak-silap-timbalan-mufti-perak

Sharom Abu Bakar. 2016. "Hadi Pertahan Tindakan Hadiri Muktamar Perpaduan Ummah di Iran". *Astro Awani.* 23 December 2016. https://www.astroawani.com/berita-malaysia/hadi-pertahan-tindakan-hadiri-muktamar-perpaduan-ummah-di-iran-126685

Siddiqui, Kallim. 1982. "The Imam Asserts the Revolution's Authority". In *Issues in the Islamic Movement 1980–'81*, edited by Kalim Siddiqui, pp. 348–51. London, Toronto and Pretoria: The Open Press Limited.

Sinar Harian. 2013a. "Semua Pertubuhan Berkaitan Syiah Dilarang". 27 July 2013. http://www.sinarharian.com.my/ultras/liga-malaysia/ semua-pertubuhan-berkaitan-syiah-dilarang-1.187288

———. 2013b, "Perlu Tapis Pelajar Luar Negara". 28 July 2013. http://www.sinarharian.com.my/perlu-tapis-pelajar-luar-negara-1.187464

———. 2013c. "Port Syiah Diserbu". 28 September 2013. http://www. sinarharian.com.my/port-syiah-diserbu-1.206383

———. 2013d. "Pelajar Sekolah Disyaki Berfahaman Syiah". 13 October

2013. http://www.sinarharian.com.my/ultras/liga-malaysia/pelajar-sekolah-disyaki-berfahaman-syiah-1.211445

———. 2013e. "Tak Mengaku Miliki Buku Syiah". 31 October 2013. http://www.sinarharian.com.my/semasa/tak-mengaku-miliki-buku-syiah-1.216144

———. 2013f. "Isma Dakwa Syiah di IPT Membimbangkan". 30 November 2013. http://www.sinarharian.com.my/semasa/isma-dakwa-syiah-di-ipt-membimbangkan-1

———. 2013g. "Abim Alu-Alukan Tindakan KDN". 14 December 2013. http://www.sinarharian.com.my/semasa/abim-alu-alukan-tindakan-kdn-1.230382

Sulaiman Noordin. 1996. "Prakata". In *Syiah Imamiyah Mazhab ke-5?* edited by Sulaiman Nordin, Mohd Zawawi Abdullah, and Mohamad Sabri Haron. Kajang: Nuur Publications.

———, Mohd Zawawi Abdullah, and Mohamad Sabri Haron, 2009. *Prosiding Seminar: Syiah Imamiyyah Mazhab ke-5?* Pusat Pengajian Umum, Universiti Kebangsaan Malaysia.

Sun Daily. 2013. "Two Enactments Adopted to Curb Shia Teachings: Jamil Khir". 2 August 2013. http://www.thesundaily.my/news/787343

Tibbetts, G.R. 1957. "Early Muslim Traders in South East Asia". *Journal of the Malayan Branch of the Royal Asiatic Society* 30, no. 1: 1–45.

TVSUNNAH. 2013. "Syiah Adalah Satu Ajaran Yang Sesat—Dato Dr MAZA". *YouTube*, 31 December 2013. https://www.youtube.com/watch?v=hxBaVMCBtCU

Utusan, Arkib. 2013a. "Kerajaan Negeri Digesa Wartakan Fatwa Anti-Syiah". 25 July 2013. http://www.utusan.com.my/utusan/Dalam_Negeri/20130725/dn_31/Kerajaan-negeri-digesa-wartakan-fatwa-anti-Syiah#ixzz2oEGieI8I

———. 2013b. "Wartakan Fatwa Anti-Syiah". 13 August 2013. http://www.utusan.com.my/utusan/Dalam_Negeri/20130813/dn_03/Wartakan-fatwa-anti-Syiah

———. 2013c. "Perak Sudah Wartakan Fatwa Anti-Syiah—Harussani". 13 August 2013. http://www.utusan.com.my/utusan/Dalam_Negeri/20130813/dn_23/Perak-sudah-wartakan-fatwa-anti-Syiah--Harussani

———. 2013d. "4 Individu Disyaki Pengikut Syiah Ditahan di Bagan

Serai". 10 September 2013. http://www.utusan.com.my/utusan/
Jenayah/20130910/je_09/4-individu-disyaki-pengikut-Syiah-
ditahan-di-Bagan-Serai

———. 2013e. "Fahaman Syiah Dilarang di Negeri Sembilan".
1 October 2013. http://www.utusan.com.my/utusan/Dalam_
Negeri/20131001/dn_53/Fahaman-Syiah-dilarang-di-Negeri-
Sembilan

Utusan Malaysia. 2009. "Waspada Tajdid Wahhabi". 7 November 2009.

———. 2010. "Markas Syiah Diserbu". 17 December 2010.

———. 2013. "Malaysia Kekal Hubungan dengan Iran".
8 September 2013. http://www.utusan.com.my/utusan/Dalam_
Negeri/20130912/dn_04/Malaysia-kekal-hubungan-dengan-Iran

———. 2016. "Asia Tenggara Sasaran Baharu Militan IS: Kronologi
Militan IS Ditahan". 19 January 2016.

Valbjørn, Morten. 2019. "What's so Sectarian about Sectarian Politics?
Identity Politics and Authoritarianism in a New Middle East".
Studies in Ethnicity and Nationalism 19, no. 1. https://onlinelibrary.
wiley.com/doi/epdf/10.1111/sena.12289

Waikar, Prashant, and Mohamed Nawab Mohamed Osman. 2020.
"The 2019 Kuala Lumpur Summit: A Strategic Realignment in
the Muslim World?". *Berkley Forum*, 24 February 2020. https://
berkleycenter.georgetown.edu/posts/the-2019-kuala-lumpur-
summit-a-strategic-realignment-in-the-muslim-world

Wan Faizal Ismayatim. 2020. "6 resolusi kekang gerakan Syiah di
Malaysia". *Berita Harian*, 5 January 2020.

Wan Zahidi Wan Teh. 1992. "Ahlul Bait Menurut Pandangan Sunnah
dan Syiah". Seminar Ahli Sunnah dan Syiah Imemiyyah, Kuala
Lumpur, 26–27 December 1992, pp. 1–34.

Wilkinson, R.J. 1957. "Papers on Malay Customs and Beliefs". *Journal
of the Malayan Branch of the Royal Asiatic Society* 30, no. 4: 1–87.

Yasmin Ramlan. 2019. "Syiah: KPM Akan Bincang Dengan Mufti".
Malaysiakini. 12 September 2019. https://www.malaysiakini.com/
news/491701

Za'ba. 2009. *Mencapai Ketinggian Dunia Akhirat*. Kuala Lumpur:
Dewan Bahasa dan Pustaka.

Zamihan Mat Zin. 2017. "Doktrin Salafiyyah Wahhabiyyah dan Respon

Umat Islam di Malaysia: Kajian Dalam Kalangan Penjawat Awam di Putrajaya dan Kuala Lumpur". PhD Thesis, National University of Malaysia, Faculty of Islamic Studies.

Zarina Othman, Nor Azizan Idris, and Abdul Halim Daud. 2020. "Pengharaman Fahaman Syiah dan Hubungan Malaysia-Iran". *Geografia Malaysian Journal of Society and Space* 16, no. 4: 117–31.

Zurairi AR. 2014, "Launched by PM But Ministry Says No Choice but to Ban Government-published 'Shiah Propaganda'". *Malay Mail*, 2 May 2014. http://www.themalaymailonline.com/malaysia/article/launched-by-pm-but-ministry-says-no-choice-but-to-ban-government-published.